Trompe L'Oeil Bible

Christopher Westall

David & Charles

In memory of my brother David

A DAVID & CHARLES BOOK

First published in the UK in 2003
Paperback edition reprinted 2003

Copyright © Christopher Westall 2003

Distributed in North America
by F&W Publications, Inc.
4700 East Galbraith Road
Cincinnati, OH 45236
1-800-289-0963

A catalogue record for this book is available from the British Library.

ISBN 0 7153 1478 5 hardback
ISBN 0 7153 1479 3 paperback (USA only)

Printed in China by Leefung-Asco
for David & Charles
Brunel House   Newton Abbot   Devon

Commissioning Editor Fiona Eaton
Desk Editor Jennifer Proverbs
Executive Art Editor Ali Myer
Designer Prudence Rogers
Production Controller Jennifer Campbell

Visit our website at www.davidandcharles.co.uk

David & Charles books are available from all good bookshops;
alternatively you can contact our Orderline on (0)1626 334555 or write to us at
FREEPOST EX2110, David & Charles Direct, Newton Abbot, TQ12 4ZZ
(no stamp required UK mainland).

Contents

Introduction

Trompe l'oeil is a French expression meaning simply 'trick the eye', and it describes a visual joke: a painted illusion, specifically designed to fool viewers into believing that what they are looking at is real. Only when they come closer to inspect the work in more detail – perhaps even as they reach over to pick up a realistically painted wine glass – do they realize to their delight that they have been duped.

The expression 'less is more' is relevant here. It is often the simple, small-scale trompe l'oeil pieces that fool more often and for longer. A small painting of a plant pot tucked away on a shelf will fool many people, as it will look perfectly natural in its situation and will not draw too much attention to itself. On the other hand, while a grandiose Arcadian landscape viewed through classical columns can be awe-inspiring to behold, we immediately realize that it is a painted illusion. However, even after the trick is discovered, the painting continues to have the desired effect of visually opening up the space in the room. And in the end we all secretly want to be found out, and receive a pat on the back for painting such a convincing illusion.

People often say to me that they wish they could paint, but feel they cannot even draw matchstick men. But with this self-defeating attitude many potential artists write themselves off before they have even dipped a brush into paint. I was a very reluctant painter myself, but I'm glad I took that first step. You may find that your initial attempts do not come up to your expectations, but do not be discouraged, as you will learn more and more each time you paint – much more, in fact, than I could hope to teach you through this book.

You may also find yourself looking in awe at other muralists' work, and envying their skill. I have been painting for over eighteen years, and I still do the same. Do look at murals by other artists for ideas and inspiration, but always be conscious that you are an individual with your own personal style, interests and aspirations – the world would be a boring, uniform place if we all painted the same way. My wish is that this book will help to spark your own artistic journey – you will be amazed at what you can achieve.

Before you begin

Before you even consider picking up a paint brush or preparing a wall for a mural, establish a clear idea of what it is you want to paint. Are you aiming to add the illusion of period architectural details to a plain room, or to create a feeling of greater space by painting a distant view? Will your mural occupy part of one wall, or transform the whole room? The function of the room may suggest themes and ideas.

The kitchen is often the hub of the home, and a place where the family regularly gathers. Because of the space taken up by kitchen cupboards, there may be little wall space on which to paint a mural. One idea would be to paint a decorative frieze along the top of a wall, such as a trailing grapevine. If a blank wall is available, a vibrant summer landscape seen through an open window would bring sunshine into the kitchen, and growing crops would give it a suitable culinary theme.

In a dining room, most of the furniture is in the centre, so there may be a lot of wall space available. This is an ideal opportunity to paint something dramatic to impress your dinner party guests. A classical theme would be popular, such as a colonnade with a view over an Arcadian landscape or a formal garden. Link the view to the room by painting a bottle of fruity red wine on a window ledge, with a half-emptied glass perched beside it.

A mural in a sitting room needs to enhance its relaxed ambience and be easy to live with. As in the kitchen, it is likely that you will usually have the top half of the wall as your canvas, because of the furniture in the room. A fireplace makes a good focal point, maybe with a painted firescreen or a decorative design on the chimney breast. Even if you have no fireplace, you could paint your own trompe l'oeil one.

If your hall is long and narrow you may have a lot of wall space, but the effect of a grand painted vista will be lost if you cannot stand back from the wall to view it. A formal and subtle stone-blocking effect could be a better solution, perhaps with a niche containing an urn on the end wall, where you and your visitors can enjoy the illusion to the full.

In the bedroom, relaxation is the key element – colours should be harmonious and restful. Here you can indulge in a touch of fantasy, such as a softly painted cloudy ceiling, with gentle drapery and fluttering cherubs. A child's bedroom is a great opportunity to kickstart your mural skills. There is a lot of satisfaction in making children's favourite characters and stories come alive on their walls. It's a good idea to involve the children in the design process, and maybe even let them help with the painting. An advantage (or disadvantage) of painting a mural for children is that they have not yet grasped the concept of diplomacy, and they will tell you straight away whether they like it or not. So if you can please them, you can please anybody!

If your bathroom is tiled, there will be little, if any, wall to paint. An alternative would be to paint a mural on a moisture-resistant board and hang it on the wall. Water themes, such as fish, leaping dolphins or the sea, are the obvious choice, but twining greenery can also create a relaxing setting. If you have the space you could surround the bath with a harmonious Roman vista, seen through columns and twisting ivy, to transport you to a classical spa as you soak.

How to use this book

The first section gives an overview of the techniques of trompe l'oeil painting, with  practical advice that will enable you to follow the detailed instructions given for the projects in the other sections. Based on four themes – Country Views, Classical Details, the Water's Edge and Children's Worlds – each section includes two step-by-step projects, as well as numerous design library pages – additional ideas for mural subjects and decorative details. Although many of the images in the design libraries form a complete picture in themselves, such as a shelf full of toys, or a view from a window, don't be afraid to mix and match different elements to create your own unique trompe l'oeil. Why not take a vase of flowers from one page, and sit them on a shelf from another? Alternatively, choose your favourite outdoor scene, and paint it as seen through any of the beautiful windows or doorways featured throughout the book. Every idea in the design libraries has practical hints and tips to help you create them, plus inspirational ideas for how and where to use them. With this book, your painting equipment and your imagination, you can create a world of illusion in every room of your home.

Techniques

Planning and Sketching

The best starting point for inspiration is yourself: your interests, your favourite flowers, where you like to go on holiday, and so on. Artists through the centuries have included personal elements in their paintings: Van Gogh's love of sunflowers inspired a series of paintings, and the painting known as *Vincent's Chair* includes his pipe, tobacco and handkerchief. When I paint a mural for clients, it is fun to add a little element that links the scene to them – maybe a bottle of their favourite wine.

Once you have some ideas for a mural, start collecting reference material. Cuttings from travel brochures could help you plan a landscape if you have a particular country in mind. Leaf through magazines for examples of elements such as windows or trees. Architectural

references for columns, balustrading and details such as urns are worth holding on to, even if you have no immediate plans to make use of them. Keep all your cuttings safe in a folder or scrapbook for future reference.

The concept sketch

Keeping your references to hand, start loosely sketching on paper with a graphite pencil to play around with different ideas. This can be a quick process, or may be long and drawn out: I admit to finding this stage one of the more difficult in the business of painting a mural. If you are struggling to translate the ideas swimming in your head into a drawing, it can be more constructive to walk away, take a break and return later with a fresher outlook.

Once the idea is on paper, you need to make accurate measurements of the area to be painted, noting dimensions of doorways, windows, radiators, sockets and switches, all of which will affect your design to some degree. Using these measurements, draw an elevation of the wall using a suitable scale (such as 10cm:1m or 1in:1ft). Use a ruler to check the scale and keep the lines

When you come to work your design on the wall, you may find you need to make slight adjustments. For example, in the concept sketch for the seagull and lighthouse design, the bird was standing on the edge of the frame. At full size this made the seagull too big for the composition, so I decided to make him smaller by placing him further back in the scene (see opposite).

straight. A calculator can also be a useful tool. It's wise to make a few copies of your accurate elevation on a photocopier or scanner before you begin to sketch your mural, so that you can try out different variations.

Sketch the main elements of the design, then use coloured pencils to build up the colouring. The level of detail is up to you – I generally keep the designs quite free and loose, as I am looking at the overall composition and colours, and how they will relate to the wall and room. Include any coloured fixtures, such as a red door, in the design so you can see how the colours will relate to one another. Finally, pick out the outlines and detailing using a black fine liner pen.

Equipment

- **Sketching paper**
- **Graphite pencils:** for sketching
- **Coloured pencils:** for trying out initial ideas for colour schemes
- **Tape measure:** to measure wall
- **Ruler:** to check scale measurements and keep lines straight
- **Calculator:** to calculate measurements to scale
- **Black fine liner pen:** to outline the final design

Surface Preparation

Surface preparation is generally regarded as a nuisance, as we would all prefer to be painting a beautiful landscape to filling cracks and sanding down the wall. However, this is arguably the most important step, as the preparation work will affect the quality of your finished painting. The amount of work needed will depend on the current state of the wall.

Wall painted with matt emulsion (latex)
This is the ideal surface for mural painting, and if the room has not been wallpapered, it is very likely to be the surface you will be dealing with. If the wall is painted white or off-white and in good repair, just wash it down with a sugar soap solution. You should then be able to proceed with the planning of the mural.

Newly plastered wall
When dry, new plaster needs to be lightly sanded and primed, either with new plaster sealer or an acrylic satin varnish, before painting it with at least two base coats of light emulsion (latex) paint.

Wallpaper
If the wallpaper is sound, matt and smooth-textured, you should be able to paint over it. Otherwise, carefully remove the paper and then make good any damage to the plaster before applying the base coats.

Oil-painted surface
If possible, strip this back using a hot air gun and scraper. You can rub down the surface and prime, but the oil-based paint will prevent air passing through the wall and will extend the drying time of the mural paints.

Cracked and chipped wall
Use an old brush to clean dust and loose plaster out of cracks, and fill with a good quality decorator's filler (spackling paste). Use the powder variety that you have to mix yourself in preference to the ready-mixed version, as it will be easier to sand down. Smooth the filler into the cracks using a filling knife, and when dry sand down with fine to medium-grade sandpaper. You may need to fill deeper cracks in two stages.

Sometimes you may not wish to repair too much damage on the wall, as it can be utilized in the design. If you are painting a rustic Italian scene with a crumbling wall, for example, blemishes and imperfections in the surface may enhance the effect.

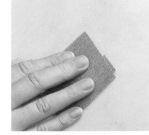

Salt deposits

These may be evidence of damp problems, which will need to be rectified. Remove the deposits with a hard brush and then prime the wall with an alkali-resistant stabilizing solution before painting.

Mould

This could also point to damp problems, so you may need to seek professional help. A common cause is condensation, so you should consider improving ventilation or installing a dehumidifier. The mould itself can be cleaned off using a specialist mould cleaner.

Panels

If the wall is damp or in very bad repair, it is worth considering painting a trompe l'oeil mural on a panel and fixing it to the wall. This has the advantage of portability: if you move home, you can take your masterpiece with you rather than leaving it to the mercy of somebody else's decorating preferences.

Panels can be made from MDF (medium density fibreboard), chipboard, hardboard, plywood, or canvas stretched on a frame. MDF is the most versatile board as it has the smoothest surface, comes in various thicknesses and is easy to cut to shape using a jigsaw. A version for exterior use is available, which is ideal for murals in bathrooms where humidity is high. Wear a mask when cutting or sanding MDF, as inhaling the dust can be harmful.

Before priming the panel, lightly rub down the surface with fine sandpaper to provide a key for the paint. The board can then be primed with an acrylic primer or a good quality emulsion (latex). This will need at least two coats – the first should be slightly watered down. Prime both sides of the panel as a precaution against warping, particularly if you are using hardboard.

Equipment

- **Stepladder:** a small aluminum stepladder will usually suffice, but if you need to hire a scaffold tower, try to get the supplying company to assemble it and instruct you on how to use and move it safely.
- **Sugar soap:** for use in solution to remove dirt and grease from surfaces before painting.
- **Sandpaper:** in a range of grades from fine to coarse, for removing flaking paint, rubbing down filler, and rubbing down panels to provide a key.
- **Plaster sealer:** for priming newly plastered walls (**acrylic satin varnish** is an alternative).
- **Hot air gun and scraper:** for removing oil-based paint.
- **Decorator's filler** (spackling paste) and **filling knife:** for repairing cracks or chips in the wall.
- **Dust sheets:** to protect floors and furniture from paint.
- **Masking tape:** to protect light switches, skirting boards, architrave etc.
- **Decorator's brushes** or **paint pads** and **paint rollers:** to apply primer and emulsion (latex) paint.

Scaling and Transferring Images

Whether you begin with your own designs, or with those in this book, they will need to be scaled up. New technology has made this aspect of the work much easier, as photocopier or computer scanners provide a very quick and easy method of copying drawings, templates and other pictorial references, scaling them up (or down) to the size you require. However, if you don't have ready access to either of these, other techniques can be used.

For the step-by-step projects in this book, the main lines of the design can be drawn straight on to the wall using the dimensions in the diagrams. When you gain more confidence in your painting you may also wish to plan landscapes straight on to the wall without first drawing them on transfer paper.

Scaling

Photocopier or computer scanner

Most photocopiers allow you to enlarge or reduce an image, setting the size in terms of a percentage of the original. A computer with a scanner and image manipulation software will give you even more control over the size of the image: an excellent feature, which I have found invaluable, is the facility to enlarge an image greatly using a method called 'tiling'. The result is printed on numerous sheets of paper, which can then be taped together like a jigsaw.

Projection

The image can be projected straight on to the wall, using either an overhead projector or an enlarger. An overhead projector requires the image to be drawn on an acetate sheet, so you will have to trace off the template first. This is not necessary with an enlarger, which is therefore less time-consuming.

Although it appears to be the most straightforward, this method does have a few hitches. First, you need to have darkness or very subdued light in the room to be able to see the projected image clearly enough to draw it. The projector must face the wall squarely, otherwise the image will be distorted, and adjusting the size of the image usually involves moving the projector further away or closer to the wall. It is advisable to project the image on to transfer paper at the size you require it, and then trace it on to the wall. Although I own an image enlarger, I rarely use it.

Grid method

This is the method that you will need to fall back on if all else fails. It involves drawing a grid over the image you wish to scale. To enlarge the image, draw a second grid to the larger scale, making sure it contains the same number of squares across the height and width as the smaller grid. Then draw the image to the larger scale, using the grid as a guide (see below).

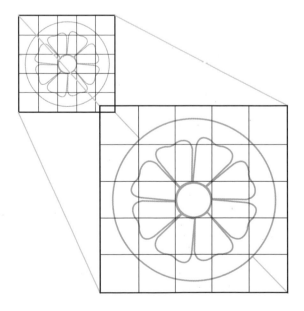

Transferring

Once you have produced your scaled-up template, either on a sheet of semi-transparent transfer paper or on ordinary photocopier or printer paper, it needs to be transferred to the wall. If you are using transfer paper, simply rub a soft graphite pencil on the back behind the outlines, then tape the sheet in place on the wall and trace over the outlines using a harder graphite pencil, to leave an imprint of the design on the wall.

This method also works with ordinary paper, although it can be difficult to see the outlines from the back of the sheet: simply rest the paper against a window in daylight so that the lines are visible. Alternatively you can use sheets of non-wax carbon paper between the design and the wall, and trace the design using a graphite pencil.

Transferring symmetrical designs

Planning and drawing objects such as a wine glass and bottle on the wall may seem a daunting task, but the template examples throughout this book have been designed to make things easier for you. If a template is symmetrical, you need only scale up half the image. Transfer this half on to the wall, then flip the paper over, line it up and trace the other half.

With symmetrical designs such as bottles and urns, you need to ensure that the images are square with the horizontals and verticals of the mural, otherwise they will appear to be leaning over. To help with this, lightly draw in a vertical guideline using a spirit level where you want the image. Align the symmetry line on the template with this vertical before tracing each side.

Rub over the back of the design with a soft pencil before taping the transfer paper in position, then draw over the outlines to leave a tracing on the wall.

Equipment

- **Tape measure:** for making accurate measurements; a steel or plastic **ruler** is useful where a tape measure would be too cumbersome, and doubles as a straight edge.
- **Spirit level:** for drawing accurate horizontals and verticals. Some levels have rotating bubbles, so that you can accurately draw angled lines. A small carpenter's level is useful for the more detailed planning; a larger level can also act as a straight edge when drawing and painting.
- **Protractor:** for measuring angles.
- **Right-angled triangle/set square:** for drawing 90° and 45° angles and for checking horizontals against verticals.
- **Charcoal and graphite pencils:** for drawing on the wall. Charcoal can be wiped off with a damp cloth; graphite is more difficult to remove, but graphite pencils have a finer point so are essential for accurate marking.
- **Eraser or putty rubber:** for removing pencil lines.
- **Semi-transparent transfer paper:** for planning designs and copying templates before transferring them to the wall; household greaseproof (waxed) paper is an alternative.
- **Carbon paper:** for transferring photocopies to the wall. If possible use a non-wax variety.
- **Masking tape:** to hold transfer paper in position.
- **Calculator:** for scaling up templates and dividing up a wall space.
- **String:** for drawing large circles and curves.
- **Pens** for drawing on **acetate:** for use with an overhead projector.

Paints and Painting

I use both good quality emulsion (latex) paint and artist's acrylics for painting murals. As both are water-based, mixing them is not a problem. Both are durable and have little odour. They also dry quickly, allowing you to build up your design gradually in layers without having to wait hours for a previous coat to dry. To paint a whole wall using purely artist's acrylic paints would be very costly, so I use matt emulsion, generally in white, to mix with the acrylic paints.

Artist's acrylic paints

These are very resilient and versatile paints. As they are water-based, thinning colours and cleaning brushes is very straightforward. The pigments are bound with polymer resin, as opposed to oil or gum: this means that the paints are very durable, do not yellow in the way that oil paints do, and as they are more porous than oil paints they are less prone to blistering.

Acrylic paints can be used thick, straight from the tube, to emulate the texture of oil paint, or thinned down with water to make a translucent wash almost like watercolour. As you will be working on vertical surfaces, it is important not to overload the brush when working with thinned paint, as it may run.

The first colour I use when starting to paint a mural is Red Oxide acrylic. After you have planned out the mural in pencil, use Red Oxide, slightly thinned with a little water, and a No. 3 or No. 5 round pointed brush to paint over all the outlines. This will ensure that you can still see the lines of the design as you start to build up the layers of colour.

Matt emulsion (latex) paint

Household matt emulsion can be used both as a base coat on the wall, and to mix with acrylic colours. Make sure you use a good quality brand of paint – buying cheap paint is a false economy, as it will generally not have the same coverage and you will need to add further coats.

Although I mainly use white emulsion, the choice of colours available in modern paint ranges is mind-boggling. Thanks to computer technology the colours do not have to be held in stock – the paint can be mixed up for you on the spot. This is very useful if your mural uses a lot of the same colour (for instance, in a blue sky) and can save you labour as well as money.

Varnish

As well as protecting the surface of the mural and prolonging its life, varnish will even out the varying lustres of acrylic and emulsion paints. I use both a satin and a flat matt acrylic varnish. First apply one or two coats of satin varnish to seal the surface. When dry, apply two to three coats of matt varnish, letting each coat dry out thoroughly before applying the next. Thin the first coats slightly with water. Apply varnish using a paint pad, as it gives a flatter, more even coating than a brush, and avoids brush marks.

Use scrunched-up plastic to create texture in wet paint (above). Build up colours in a distant view (below) starting with blues and blending into greens, intensifying the colours toward the foreground.

Equipment

- **Decorator's brush:** 13cm (5in) wide, for applying base coats, colourwashing and painting large areas such as skies.
- **Nylon artist's brushes:** range from round pointed tips for more detailed work, to wide flat shapes for blocking in colours. These are relatively inexpensive and of a reasonable quality; sable brushes are more expensive, but will long outlive nylon brushes if looked after properly.
- **Hog-hair varnishing brushes:** for blending in larger areas of colour (rather than applying varnish). Also excellent for stippling in foliage effects. They eventually become worn and chiselled, but are still useful for stippling effects.
- **Paint pad:** for applying varnish smoothly and evenly.
- **Plastic cups:** for mixing and holding paint. If possible, use cups with lids to stop paints drying out when not in use. Use plastic spoons to spoon emulsion paint out of its tub. Use old artist's brushes to mix the paint.
- **Permanent maker pen:** to label plastic cups containing mixed colours. Useful when using various shades of the same colour (such as graduating sky blues). It can be difficult to see whether one colour is darker than another until they have dried on the wall.
- **Low-tack masking tape:** for painting crisp straight edges. I do not advocate excessive use of masking tape for this purpose, but when painting subjects such as trellis or railings it would be difficult not to use it. The paint surface must be sound as, if it is not, some paint may be lifted when the masking tape is removed later. Use short brush strokes, working out from the tape to avoid paint seeping underneath.
- **Plastic bags:** used to create a rough stony texture. Try dabbing, rolling and rubbing a bag over the wet painted surface to achieve different effects. When the bag gets overloaded with paint, discard it and use a fresh one.

Understanding Perspective

Creating the perception of a real three-dimensional space on a two-dimensional surface is the challenge for all trompe l'oeil artists. Filippo Brunelleschi, a 15th-century architect, formulated mathematical laws that can be applied to spatial relationships, and these allow us to create believable illusions of space beyond a flat surface.

An understanding of the basic rules of perspective is vital for creating convincing three-dimensional trompe l'oeil on a two-dimensional surface. When planning a mural it is vital that you work out the correct perspective first, as a mistake at this stage can be very difficult to rectify when you are halfway through the painting. It quickly becomes obvious if the perspective is not correct: for example, a patio in the foreground of a garden scene might look as if it is going uphill, rather than lying level. Slight errors are difficult to spot while you are working on the wall, as your eye becomes adjusted to them. Try looking at the reflected image of the mural in a mirror – this will give you a fresh view, and instantly show up any areas that need attention.

One-point perspective

Imagine standing in the middle of a straight level railway track (do not try this for real!). Looking along the track, you will notice that the two rails seem to move closer and closer together the further away they are. The railway sleepers also appear closer to each other (see diagram above right). When the two rails reach the horizon, they appear to meet – the point where they meet is referred to as the vanishing point. Imagine a line of trees running parallel to the track – they will also diminish in size as they near the vanishing point.

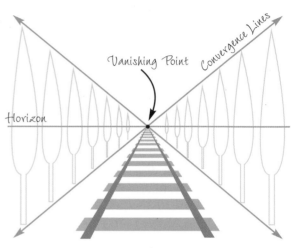

One-point Perspective

The horizon line and eye level

In general, the vanishing point is located on the horizon line. Imagine looking out across the sea to the distant horizon (below), where the sea and sky meet. This line will always appear to be at your eye level, whether you are standing or sitting, are on the beach or on a cliff top.

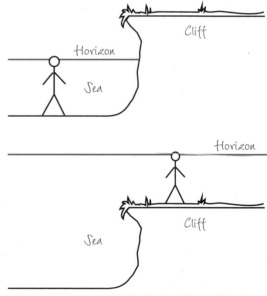

The Horizon Line and Eye Level

Establishing the horizon line is one of the first steps when planning a mural. To foster the illusion that you are looking into the distance, it needs to be placed on the wall at around the actual level of your eyes. My own eye level is at a height of about 173cm (5ft 8in), but because my murals will also be viewed by shorter people I plan a compromise horizon line to accommodate lower eye levels. If you are painting a mural that will normally be viewed from a sitting position, an even lower horizon line may be more effective.

The horizon line is the starting point for planning a distant landscape – any mountains or highlands will be above the line. However, there will be occasions when using the true horizon line would mean that little room would be left for an area of sky. In such cases, a degree of compromise is again required, and the rules may have to be bent slightly in favour of aesthetics.

Drawing convergence lines

The lines of the railway track are convergence lines: when parallel lines run away from the viewer, they will always meet at the vanishing point on the horizon. Similarly, if you stand in a room and face the far wall squarely, you will see that the edges of the floor and ceiling appear to be at an angle and to be leading toward the same point.

To help plan these converging lines in your mural, the first step is to establish the vanishing point. Once you have done this, a piece of string will suddenly become one of the most invaluable tools at your disposal. Simply fix a suitable length to the vanishing point using masking tape. Use three pieces of tape for this: the first piece holds the string in place, and two further pieces immediately to each side of the vanishing point stop the string slipping or the first piece of tape lifting away. You should be able to move the string in all directions without it slipping from the vanishing point, otherwise your measurements will be inaccurate.

The string can now be used to plan all the one-point perspective convergence lines in your mural, such as the edges of paving slabs, the inside edges of archways, windows and doorways, and other architectural features in your design. Hold the string firmly so it is taut (but not so taut that it is pulled from the wall) and mark off points along the string with a pencil. Draw each convergence line along these points using a straight edge.

In this picture the converging lines of the doors, louvres and patio slabs would all meet at the vanishing point on the distant horizon. See page 41 for another example of convergance lines.

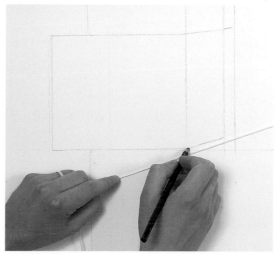

Use three pieces of tape to hold one end of the string at the vanishing point, so that you can move it in any direction without pulling it away from the wall. Hold the other end firmly while you mark the convergence lines.

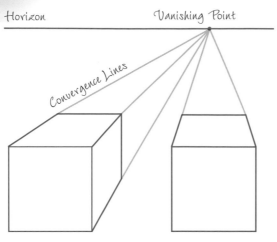

Horizon Vanishing Point

Convergence Lines

Two-point Perspective (A)

While the vanishing point for one-point perspective is straightforward to establish, two-point perspective can present problems. The vanishing points may be at quite a distance along the horizon line, and you will often find that there is not enough wall space to mark one of them in. In the Provençal Landscape project (page 28), the front edges of the louvred doors each have a separate vanishing point, but rather than try to establish these, which would be a fair distance from the mural, I simply drew the short converging lines by eye.

Two-point perspective

Imagine a cube-shaped block. If it is directly in front of you, and below the vanishing point, you will be able to see the top of the block, with the sides converging toward the vanishing point, but the edges of the front face will be horizontal and vertical (see diagram A, above). If the block is moved to the left of the vanishing point, you will see some of the right-hand side, but the front face will still be square.

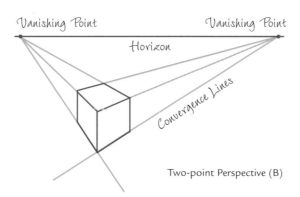

Vanishing Point Vanishing Point

Horizon

Convergence Lines

Two-point Perspective (B)

Now imagine that the block is turned round slightly (see diagram B, above). The top and bottom edges of the front, which were horizontal, will now appear as converging lines, with a vanishing point on the horizon line to one side of the block. The other visible face has a separate vanishing point, again on the horizon line. The block no longer has a centre vanishing point.

Three-point perspective.

If the block were extremely tall, like a skyscraper, the vertical sides would also appear to be converging toward a third vanishing point above it. However, it is very unlikely that you would ever need to resort to using three vanishing points, unless you need to exaggerate a great height or depth in your mural – generally, all your vertical lines will stay vertical.

Reflections

If an object is reflected in water, the reflection will share the same vanishing points as the object, and the depth of the reflection should equal the height of the object. If the reflected object is actually in the water (such as a boat) or right at its edge, the reflection will begin at the foot of the object.

An object such as a building or a tree is more likely to be standing further away from the water's edge. However, the line of reflection remains at the foot of the object and the depth of the reflection should still be measured from here. If the object is situated higher up – on a river bank, for instance – there will be a vertical distance between its foot and the surface of the water. The depth of the reflection will equal this vertical height plus the height of the object.

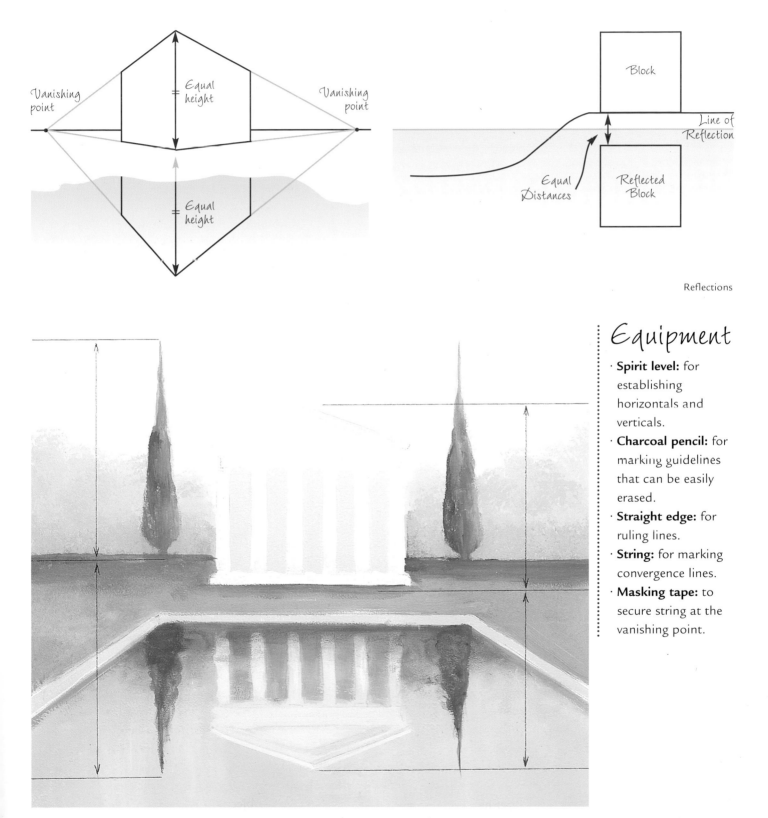

Vanishing point

Equal height

Vanishing point

Equal height

Block

Line of Reflection

Equal Distances

Reflected Block

Reflections

Equipment

- **Spirit level:** for establishing horizontals and verticals.
- **Charcoal pencil:** for marking guidelines that can be easily erased.
- **Straight edge:** for ruling lines.
- **String:** for marking convergence lines.
- **Masking tape:** to secure string at the vanishing point.

Using Colour

Entire books have been written concerning colour theory, but only brief notes are possible here. Sir Isaac Newton, who used a prism to separate daylight into its constituent colours, developed the colour wheel in 1704, and a basic understanding of the wheel is helpful when choosing and mixing colours.

The three primary colours are red, yellow and blue. In theory, using these three colours in their purest form, any colour in the spectrum can be produced. Secondary colours, shown between the primaries on the wheel, are produced by mixing two of the three primary colours together. Mixing red and blue produces violet, blue and yellow together produce green, and yellow and red produce orange.

Complementary colours

The use of complementary colours is a visual trick that artists have been playing for centuries. Colours that are opposite each other on the colour wheel have the effect of enhancing each other. For example, a ripe tomato will appear a more vibrant red if it is placed on a green cloth, an orange will seem more striking against a blue sky, and so on.

As an experiment, paint two small areas of colour – one in blue and one in red. Now paint an orange circle in the middle of each. The orange circle in the blue area will look much sharper and bolder than the circle in the red area, even though the strength of the orange is the same in both (see left, top and bottom).

Mixing two complementary colours will tend to give browny-grey tones, because opposite colours neutralize each other. This can be useful for mixing shadow tones, and is more effective than adding black to create a shadow, as this will only dirty the colour. (As an exception to this rule, I do sometimes add a little black, or even Paynes Grey, to Chromium Oxide Green to make a deeper green.)

Harmonious colours

These are the colours that sit next to each other on the colour wheel, such as the greens and blues, or the yellows and oranges. They can be used to create a more relaxing scene, in which the colours do not have the effect of pulling you in opposite directions.

This painting uses mainly cool blues and greens. The red lighthouse offers the only striking visual element to complement the harmonious colours.

Warm and cool colours

Red, orange and yellow, on one side of the colour wheel, are the warm colours that we associate with fire, while green, blue and violet on the other side are the cool colours that we associate with snow. However, if you compare different tones of any colour, you will see that there are warm and cool versions of it.

Greys and neutrals

If you mix the three primary colours together in equal strengths you will get a true grey. In unequal strengths, they give a coloured neutral. These neutrals and greys are much more versatile than the grey obtained by mixing Black and White. When painting skies, I usually mix Cobalt Blue with White for a general sky blue; by adding some Flesh Tint I can create a subtle pinky grey that is ideal for adding shadows to clouds.

Aerial or colour perspective

The use of colour can help to suggest distance in a mural. If you look over a landscape you will see that the distant hills and foliage take on a hazy bluish tinge, and may appear only a shade darker than the sky. This is due to the moisture and dust particles present in the atmosphere. The more distant an object, the more atmosphere you have to look through to see it, and the more faded its colour will appear. A tree in the foreground will be a more vibrant green, with more visible detail, than one in the distance. If the distant elements in your mural look too defined, try painting over a light blue colourwash to 'knock back' the colours and blur the edges.

The colour palette

If you flick through this book, you will see that I generally use the same basic paint colours for every project. This is the palette I have grown used to and as a rule I can use it to mix any colour I need, rather than using a different tube of paint. Using a limited palette is a good discipline, and it has the effect of harmonizing the whole painting, because the acrylic colour used to mix the sky tones, for example, will be the same one that was used to mix the colours for the mountains and trees. Over time you will build up your own personal palette of colours that you feel comfortable working with.

The rich colours and strong contrasts used in this mural help to evoke the brightness and warmth of a summer's day.

Tips on mixing colours

· If you are likely to need a lot of a particular colour, mix more than you think you will need and keep it in an airtight container to stop it drying out. Mixing exactly the same shade again is nearly impossible. Alternatively, mix up a tester shade of the colour you need, paint some on to a card and take it to a paint supplier to get as close a match as possible.

· When mixing very dark colours, like Paynes Grey or Cobalt Blue, into a lighter colour, put some of the dark colour in a separate pot and gradually mix in about 3–4 parts water. Gradually add this to the lighter colour in another pot, mixing the paint as you go, until you get the desired colour.

· When testing colours on the wall, bear in mind that the colour will alter slightly as the paint dries, and will generally be darker when wet. A hair dryer can be useful to dry paint quickly.

· If you need to match a colour on the wall, cut a square hole in the centre of a small piece of white card. Mix the colour you think will fit and paint it over the card. When the paint has dried, hold the card up to the wall and look at the two shades – this should give you a indication of how close your colour match is and how to amend it.

Applying Light and Shadow

When light is cast on to an object, the shadows, highlights and tonal values that are created describe the object's form. In trompe l'oeil, the use of light and shadow has a vital role in rendering believable three-dimensional objects.

Light source

Before you can model an object using highlights and shadows, you need to establish the direction of the light source. If the wall you are working on has a window to the left or right then it makes sense to use this as the light source for your painting. If the mural depicts an open window, the main source of light will be from the perceived daylight coming through the window. This will have the effect of highlighting the inside return of the window frame – even the top. Do not feel that as the sun is high in the sky the top return of the window should be in shadow: it will be highlighted by reflected light – if in doubt, look at a real window in daylight from inside to see what I mean.

Cast shadows

If you are painting a trompe l'oeil scene, such as an urn in a garden, think about the time of day you are trying to recreate and therefore what the sun's position in the sky would be. At midday in the summer, the sun would be high in the sky so the cast shadows would be short and sharply defined. Early or late in the day, the light would be weaker and the shadows longer. They would be more defined near the base of the urn, softer and more blurry toward their ends.

The best way to appreciate how light affects an object is through observation: look at objects at different times of the day, and even in artificial light. It is equally important to observe

Subtle shading on the terracotta pot contrasts with the sharp highlights on the glazed vase.

the colours in the cast shadows – they are seldom grey. Shadows on white surfaces, for example, can take on a subtle blue-grey colour, or may sometimes even be pinkish. Sometimes you can use some of the complementary colour of the object in its cast shadow – for example, adding a purple tinge to the colour of the shadow cast by a bunch of bananas.

If the surface on which the shadow falls is a different colour, such as red, you will need to add its complementary colour, green, to make a shadow tone. Look at the real shadows cast on the wall and try to match the colour – this involves a lot of trial and error so I suggest experimenting on another part of the wall until you feel the colour is right.

Conveying the solidity of a subject such as this urn and pedestal depends entirely on the depiction of light and shadow playing on the stone.

this is to look at a black and white photograph. In the absence of colour, you can see how the light is affecting the tonal values of different objects. You will also notice how different shapes and surfaces are affected by the light, and the transitions between tones. For example, a spherical object will have smoother gradations of tone than an angular object, and a polished surface has sharper highlights than a matt surface.

When painting these tones, you can simplify them down to a medium tone, or base colour, a shadow tone and a highlight tone. Both the shadow and highlight tones should be mixed from the base colour.

The smooth, curved surface of this ball (above) calls for subtle gradations of tone, while sharp highlights and shadows define the angular contours and hard, shiny surfaces of a child's toy bucket and spade (left).

Tone

Tonal values are the different grades of a single colour that come about when light is cast over an object. If you look at a yellow ball in sunlight, you will see that on the part of the ball facing the light the yellow is almost white. As the ball's surface curves away from the light, the colour deepens. A very bright light would give dramatic changes in tone, and a more diffused light would give a more subtle gradation of tone. The best way to appreciate

Clouds can be added, with the flat brush, by using some of the lighter blues and painting the top edge of the colour, then blending downward. Repeating this and overlapping the cloud shapes will give the sky a feeling of depth. A little white can be added to the cloud tips as a highlight.

Special Painting Techniques

The detailed instructions for the projects in this book include plenty of hints on achieving realistic-looking textures and effects in trompe l'oeil, but some elements crop up in many different contexts, and it is well worth mastering some of the tried and tested techniques that will turn your paintings into really convincing illusions. Expert sky, cloud and foliage effects will give depth to landscapes, while ageing techniques are applied to give interest to the painted surface itself.

Skies

If you look at the sky on a clear day you will see that the blue is deepest in the highest part, and lightens toward the distant horizon, to a very pale blue that is almost white. Early in the morning the sky may be a light ochre yellow near the horizon, while a subtle pinky tinge to the horizon will suggest the end of the day.

I use Cobalt Blue and Coeruleum Blue mixed into White to make sky blues. Mix at least three shades, graduating them from light to dark, and thin them slightly with water to help the colours blend together more easily. Using a flat brush, paint the sky in horizontal strokes, working from the top down to the horizon. Begin with the darkest shade, and work through to the lighter shades, blending the colours as you go.

Foliage

The different colours and textures of leaves are very useful in suggesting depth in a mural. The trees and shrubs in the foreground will show the strongest colours and highest contrasts, and clumps of foliage can be indicated by stippling with a flat brush. Further away, the colours will appear softer and bluer, until they almost merge with the distant hills or the sky.

To reproduce a warm late afternoon sky, White mixed with a little Flesh Tint is blended up from the horizon into the lighter blues, and is also used to tint the bottom of the clouds.

Depth is created in this hazy landscape by stippling in the mid-ground foliage and distant trees in a range of blue tones. Further forward in the mural more greens are added, so that the bold foliage stands out against the subtle blues and jades of the distant trees.

This olive tree has been built up in stippled layers. The tree trunk and branches are painted using Raw Umber mixed with Paynes Grey. The green base colour is Chromium Oxide Green with a little Paynes Grey. Mid-green, a mixture of White, Chromium Oxide Green, Flesh Tint and a little Cobalt Blue, is first stippled along the top edge of the tree and then blended down. This can be repeated to highlight other prominent parts of the foliage. Further highlights can be picked out in light green, mixed from White, Chromium Oxide Green and Naples Yellow, which is then blended into the mid-green. If the effect begins to look too dense, patches of the background colours can be stippled between the foliage to break it up slightly.

Ageing effects

Ancient frescos, like the leaping dolphins that adorn the walls of the Queen's Apartment in the Cretan Palace of Knossos, hold a great fascination. Much of their charm lies in their fragility, as the passing centuries have crumbled away parts of the the fresco surface. If you want to echo the soft colours and pitted surface of an ancient wall you can either leave your mural to age naturally for the next few thousand years – or try a few shortcuts to achieve the impression of age.

Vandalizing your work in such a manner may seem daunting, but the results will be worth it. It is a good idea to practise the techniques first on a sample board or another wall, particularly those that involve painting over your mural.

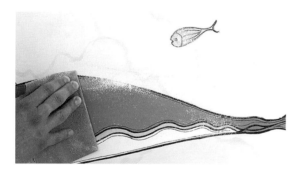

1 First distress the surface of the mural in random areas, using medium-grade sandpaper – use different motions to see what effects can be achieved. Try rubbing away a small area of solid colour, then painting over it again in one light coat – this will give a subtle patchy effect to the colour.

2 Make up a wash using 1 part Raw Umber and 7 parts water. Brush this colour over random areas of the wall using a large decorator's brush, ensuring that you brush out any paint runs. This will have the effect of dirtying the mural, so do not overdo it. Use a wet cloth to rub off some of the colour in a few areas. Repeat this as desired, and above all experiment.

3 Mix Naples Yellow with White and add a small amount of Raw Umber and Paynes Grey. Add little or no water, as the paint needs to be reasonably thick. Using a 15mm (5/8in) flat brush, paint a diagonal crack, adjusting the pressure and angle of the brush to control the width of the line. As you reach the edge of the mural, open the crack out so that it forks, creating little islands of broken fresco. Keep the edges sharp and angular, occasionally rounding the odd edge here and there. The 'missing' parts of the mural need to be completely blotted out, so keep building up the layers of paint.

4 Add a little more Raw Umber and Paynes Grey to some of the colour to make a shadow tone. Using a No. 5 round pointed brush, pick out the sharp cast shadows in the areas you have painted out, to create the illusion that the areas of missing fresco are recessed into the wall. In some areas, the edges where the light would fall can be slightly highlighted using Naples Yellow and White with a No. 3 round pointed brush.

Country Views

Thoughts of the countryside can summon up a host of different images: we might envisage a vibrant carpet of bluebells, with their delicate scent wafted on the spring breeze, a babbling brook, a crumbling villa flanked by cypress trees, the vivid greens and sky blues of a lazy summer, or the golden browns of fallen leaves as the end of the year approaches. Even a countryside scene frozen under a covering of snow can fill us with warmth.

A view of open space and natural beauty is a constant pleasure, providing an escape from towns and cities, steel and concrete, into a simpler way of life away from the pressures of modern living. But if you don't have the countryside just outside your window, a painted view of your favourite rural scene can lift your spirits even on the dullest days.

For the best effect, link the scene outside to your own interior by framing it in a doorway or window, softened with curtains or shutters, or perhaps a trailing plant – even a grapevine. If you are painting a windowsill, add a vase of country flowers that look as if you have just picked them in the fields outside.

Provençal Landscape

THE DIVERSE LANDSCAPE of this region of southern France has a rich palette of colours, blending fields of golden wheat with rows of lavender, vineyards and orchards growing cherries, peaches and apricots. These beautiful, sunlit vistas inspired Van Gogh and his contemporaries to capture the essence of the Provençal landscape on canvas.

The feeling of depth in this mural is created by the use of perspective on the window shutters, the receding rows of lavender, the cool blue of the hills and the pale jade greens of the distant trees. Bold colours are used for the foreground elements – the terracotta-washed wall, yellow shutters and purple lavender – helping them to leap forward in the mural. Sunlight is suggested by the strong shadows cast by the shutters, and the contrast between the sunlit and shaded walls of the distant farmhouse.

Experiment with variations of the scene and colours (see pages 40–43 for inspiration). You might prefer a sand-coloured wall, with green or jade shutters, or you could change the scene entirely, perhaps to a view of Tuscan, Basque or Scandinavian countryside.

Provençal Landscape 29

Palette

Red Oxide

Yellow Ochre

Raw Umber

White

Flesh Tint

Burnt Sienna

Cadmium Yellow

Windsor Violet

Raw Sienna

Cobalt Blue

Coeruleum Blue

Chromium Oxide Green

Paynes Grey

Leaf Green

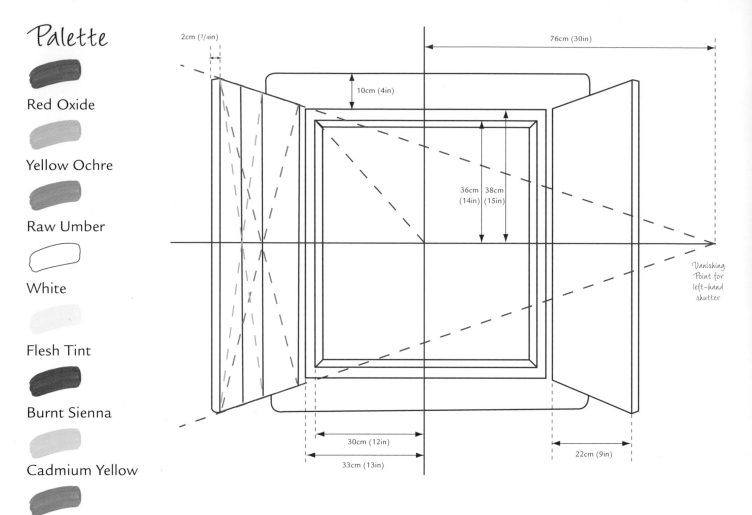

2cm (³/₄in)

76cm (30in)

10cm (4in)

36cm (14in) | 38cm (15in)

Vanishing Point for left-hand shutter

30cm (12in)

33cm (13in)

22cm (9in)

1 Using a spirit level and charcoal pencil, lightly draw in the centre vertical and the horizon line to establish the centre vanishing point. Measuring from these guidelines, draw the rest of the window frame referring to the diagram. To draw the short receding lines at the inner corners of the frame, position a straight edge so it intersects the centre vanishing point.

Draw the inner edges of the shutter doors about 1.5cm (⁵/₈in) from the window frame to allow space for the hinges, which should be about 10cm (4in) from the top and bottom of the shutters. Different vanishing points are needed to draw the shutters as they are open at an angle to the wall. Measure 76cm (30in) from the centre along the horizon on each side. Fix a length of string to the first point to mark the positions for the top and bottom edges, and the hinges, of the opposite shutter, then repeat on the other side.

As the horizon line passes through the middle of the window, the receding angles of the top and bottom edges of the shutters are identical. In reality the shutters would each be about 33cm (13in) wide, but as they are viewed at an angle they appear foreshortened and are drawn at about 22cm (9in) wide. Use a length of masking tape to help establish the position of each outer edge, standing back to check it by eye, then draw in the vertical to meet the two diverging lines. Draw parallel verticals for the edges of the shutters, which are 2cm (³/₄in) thick; the lines at the top and bottom of the edges should slope slightly from the horizontal.

To divide each shutter into planks, draw diagonals from the corners and draw a vertical where they intersect. Repeat with each section to divide the shutter into four. When drawing in the hinges, ensure that they extend over all the planks and follow the same vanishing point used for the door.

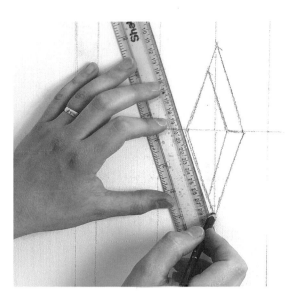

2 Position the diamond cutouts in the centre of the shutters by measuring 8cm (3in) above and below the horizon line for the top and bottom of the diamond. Mark the two side points in the middle of the width of each plank, and join the points to make the diamond. Draw a 2cm (3/4in) line horizontally from the inner corner of the diamond, then draw the two inner diagonal lines parallel to the outer lines, to represent the thickness of the shutter.

3 Paint in the outlines of the frame, shutters and hinges, using dilute red oxide paint and a No. 5 round pointed brush. Use a spirit level to guide the brush. Indicate some ageing and random splitting of the wood. Divide the stone frame into three at the top and bottom, and paint in the joints, kinking the vertical lines inward on the inner part of the frame in line with the centre vanishing point.

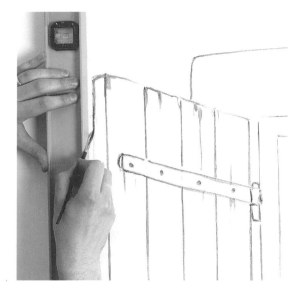

4 Attach a sheet of transfer paper to the area inside the window and draw in the horizon line established in step 1. Draw the main elements of the design using the illustration, or your own preliminary sketches, as reference. Keep the distant highlands above the horizon line and the foreground below. To help with the perspective of the lavender rows, use string taped halfway between the centre vanishing point and the right hand side of the window on the horizon line, but avoid drawing the lines too straight. When you are happy with the composition transfer the design on to the wall.

5 Paint in the landscape outlines in Red Oxide, using Nos. 3 and 5 round pointed brushes, and adding further details as you go. Mix up a colourwash using Yellow Ochre, Raw Umber and White mixed with about 4–5 parts water. Test the wash on a small area to ensure you are happy with the colour, then wash it over the whole mural using a large decorator's brush. Leave to dry and repeat if necessary.

6 Mix up a terracotta colour using Flesh Tint, Burnt Sienna and White, mixed with about 2 parts water. Using a 25mm (1in) hog-hair brush, paint the area outside the window frame (use the large decorator's brush if you are carrying this colour over a large wall area). Aim to achieve the effect of an aged terracotta wall, applying the colour unevenly and thinning it in places with the wash used in step 5. The effect can be finalized with further coats later.

7 For the shutters, mix Cadmium Yellow Deep Hue with a little White and 1 part water. For a deeper shadow tone, mix some of this colour with a little Windsor Violet and Raw Sienna. Use a 25mm (1in) hog-hair brush and a 15mm (5/8in) flat brush to block in the doors using vertical strokes. Leave the paint patchy in places to give a weathered effect. As the light source is to the right, the left-hand door will catch more light than the right, so paint this lighter, with the edge in shadow. The right-hand door should be painted in the slightly darker tone.

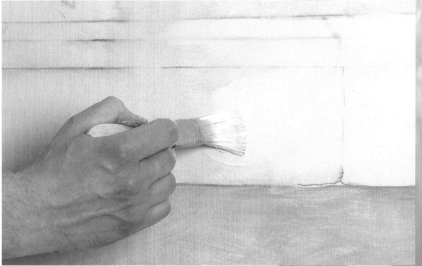

8 For the window frame, mix Raw Umber and White with 1 part water. Add some Flesh Tint to make a second, warmer stone colour. Use a 25mm (1in) hog-hair brush and a 15mm (5/8in) flat brush to brush and stipple the two colours to create a stone effect.

9 Mix Cobalt Blue, Coeruleum Blue and White, with 1 part water, to give three varying shades of blue (the lightest blue should be nearly white). Using a 15mm (⁵/₈in) flat brush, paint the sky, starting from the top with the deepest blue, and working downwards using horizontal strokes. Switch to the lighter blues as you work down toward the mountains, blending the colours as you go. Repeat until you get a smooth gradation of colour.

10 Loosely block in the distant mountains using a 15mm (⁵/₈in) flat brush and a mix of Cobalt Blue, White and a little Burnt Sienna, with 1 part water. Allow the yellow wash to show through slightly, to give the colour a pleasing texture. Try also mixing in some of the sky blue colours to vary the tones.

11 Mix two shades of jade green using Cobalt Blue, Chromium Oxide Green and White, with 1 part water. Use Nos. 3 and 5 round pointed brushes to block in the mid-ground trees and foliage, again leaving a patchy texture. Build up the shade on the farmhouse using some of the terracotta wall colour and the deeper sky blue. Leave the walls facing the light source unpainted, to give the buildings form.

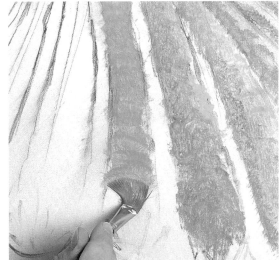

12 Mix two shades of lavender using Windsor Violet and White. Use a 15mm (⁵/₈in) flat brush to stipple the colour down each row of lavender, pushing the brush into the wall so that it fans out. As the light is coming from the right, keep the darker shade to the left of the rows. Note that where you see the lavender rows head on, the gaps between them are visible, but they are gradually obscured as you look across the rows.

Provençal Landscape 33

13 Returning to the stone window frame, mix a dark stone colour using Flesh Tint, Cobalt Blue, Paynes Grey and a little White, with 1 part water. Using Nos. 3 and 5 round pointed brushes, pick out the deep shadows in the joints between the stones, next to the shutter and in the inner recess of the frame. Mix White with a little of the original stone colour mixed in step 8 to pick out the highlights at the top of the frame, and around the recess. Create chips in the stone by smudging the darker tone in places and adding a highlight to the bottom left of the smudge.

14 Boldly defined shadows cast by the shutters suggest strong sunlight. With the light source from the upper right, the shadows are cast toward the bottom left. The shadow cast by the right-hand door is shorter, but the bottoms of both shadows should line up horizontally, as both doors are open at the same angle. Use masking tape lightly to help you plan where the shadows should fall, re-applying it until you are happy with their angle and length. Sketch in the edge of the shadow and remove the tape.

15 Mix up a shadow tone by adding Cobalt Blue to some of the wall colour mixed in step 6, and paint it on using a 25mm (1in) hog-hair brush and a 15mm (5/8in) flat brush, not forgetting to paint inside the diamond cutouts. Paint the shadow over the window frame using the dark stone colour mixed in step 13.

16 For the shadows on the shutters, mix a deeper yellow with Cadmium Yellow and Windsor Violet, with a small amount of White and a little water. Use a No. 3 round pointed brush to pick out the deep shadows between the planks. Paint shallow shadows underneath the hinges and bring out the detail by adding highlights at the top, using White mixed with a little Cadmium Yellow. Pick out highlights on the tops of the doors and along the planks. Deeper yellows can also be used to suggest a woodgrain effect.

17 Mix Chromium Oxide Green with a little Paynes Grey, and use Nos. 3 and 5 round pointed brushes to strengthen the greens of the mid-ground trees, darkening the colour toward the bottom. Mix in some Leaf Green and stipple some more vibrant foliage using a 10mm (³/₈in) flat brush. Mix some of the deep sky blue colour with a little more Cobalt Blue, and use this to add some deep blue foliage behind the trees, to build up the feeling of depth.

18 Sketch the large tree on the right lightly in charcoal. Mix Raw Umber with Paynes Grey, with 1 part water, and use Nos. 1, 3 and 5 round pointed brushes to build up the structure of the tree, with the trunk splitting into branches and then into smaller branches and twigs. Keep a suitable reference nearby.

19 Use 15mm (⁵/₈in) and 10mm (³/₈in) flat brushes to stipple the foliage of the tree. First use Chromium Oxide Green to flesh out the skeleton, leaving random gaps in the foliage. Paint in the trunk and branches again where necessary, before stippling on a lighter colour using a mixture of Leaf Green, Chromium Oxide Green and White. Leave some of the deeper green visible to help create depth in the foliage.

20 Use the yellows of the shutters and shadow tones to build up layers of grass in the foreground, to obscure the ends of the lavender rows. Using a 15mm (⁵/₈in) flat brush, apply the paint in short upward sweeps. Blend in some of the greens in places to break up the yellow. Look over the whole mural again and tweak the details or build up the colours where necessary.

Wisteria Trellis

TREILLAGE, OR THE ART OF TRELLISWORK – using a latticework of wooden struts to create elegant garden features – has been around since the fourteenth century. It has been used to erect elaborate structures that echo grand architectural forms, but these days trelliswork is most often used more simply, fixed to a wall to act as a support for climbing plants.

In this mural, the trellis provides a well-structured yet light and airy support for the climbing wisteria, providing a delicately coloured setting for the dangling flowers. Its open centre allows a clear view of the blue sky, and through the structure can be seen a tantalizing glimpse of the landscape beyond. The wall to be painted can be white or off-white.

This small-scale project looks effective on its own, but it could also be combined with other ideas: a trellis archway with climbing plants could lead into an idyllic country garden, or a trellis frieze could be painted along the top of a wall, with a climbing plant weaving in and out of it, such as the ivy or grapevines on pages 44–45.

Palette

Raw Umber

White

Flesh Tint

Naples Yellow

Windsor Violet

Cobalt Blue

Coeruleum Blue

Chromium Oxide Green

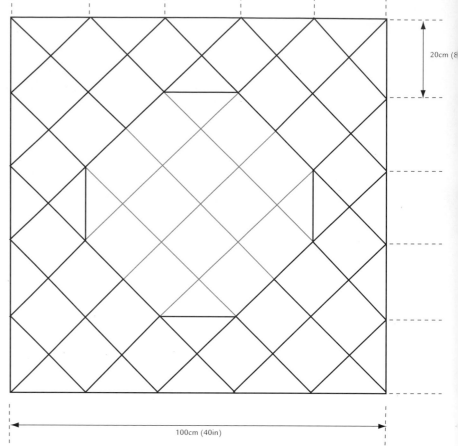

100cm (40in)

20cm (8

100cm (40in)

1 Using a spirit level and charcoal pencil, measure out a 100cm (40in) square at about window height on the wall. Divide each of the four sides into five 20cm (8in) sections. Lightly join up the points with diagonal lines, following the diagram, to form the grid pattern for the trellis.

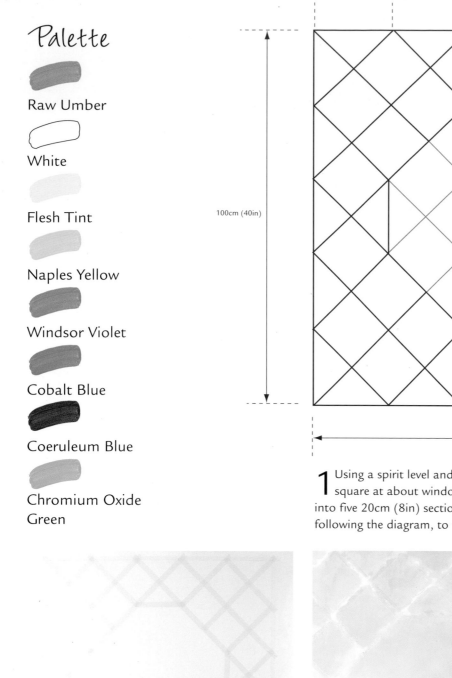

2 Using low-tack masking tape 2.5cm (1in) wide, tape over the diagonal charcoal lines, leaving a window in the centre. Also mask off the four sides of the outer square. Be careful not to lift flakes of paint when you remove the tape. Test an area first, and if the painted surface is unsuitable for masking tape, paint the design onto a panel which can be mounted onto the wall when finished.

3 Mix three or four sky blues, using varying proportions of White, Cobalt Blue and Coeruleum Blue. Keep the paint reasonably thick, adding only a small amount of water, if any, to avoid paint seeping under the tape, and use a 25mm (1in) hog-hair brush, working outward from the tape in short strokes. Blend the colours from darkest at the top to lightest at the bottom, and repeat this step two or three times to get the desired effect. Finally, add some simple clouds in the middle, using the lighter blue and blending the colour downward.

4 Mix one shade of green using Chromium Oxide Green and a little White, and a second, darker shade using Chromium Oxide Green, Cobalt Blue and a little White. Using a 15mm (⁵/₈in) flat brush and the darker green, loosely paint some foliage along the bottom and a little way up the sides of the trellis. Gradually blend this colour upward into the paler green, and then into the deeper sky blue. Create vague leaf shapes using simple, short brush strokes.

5 Mix two greeny browns, using Raw Umber, Chromium Oxide Green, Naples Yellow and a little White. Using Nos. 5 and 7 round pointed brushes, paint the wisteria stems coming in from about a quarter of the way up each side and winding up and over the trellis, gradually tapering the stems.

6 Use a No. 3 round pointed brush to add the smaller stems that will bear the leaves, curving them slightly downward. Add even smaller stems growing out equally on each side, again curving down. Using the greens mixed in step 4 and a No. 5 round pointed brush, paint the long pointed leaves using the small stems to guide you.

7 Paint similar fine stems for the flowers, about 18cm (7in) long, hanging down from the main stem and slightly curved. Mix two shades using White, Windsor Violet and Coeruleum Blue, and paint the flowers using Nos. 3 and 5 round pointed brushes. Follow a simple inverted teardrop shape for each flower panicle, wide at the top and tapering at the bottom, curving it to follow the shape of the stem. Use simple short brush strokes for the individual flowers.

8 Work over the mural again to enhance any areas that need bringing out more, such as deepening some of the foliage at the bottom. When the paint is completely dry, carefully remove the masking tape and wipe off the charcoal guidelines. Mix a pinky grey shadow tone using White, Flesh Tint and Cobalt Blue. Using a No. 3 round pointed brush, paint thin cast shadows to the lower right of each intersection so that it appears that the trellis is overlapping. A small blob of shadow tone in the middle of each intersection gives the appearance that the trellis is nailed together. Add more leaves and flowers hanging in front of the trellis (mix some slightly lighter greens and violets for this), and use the shadow tone to paint the shadows they cast.

DOORS OPENING outward to reveal a trompe l'oeil view create the feeling of space within a small room, and will leave the viewer curious to discover what is beyond them. The doors could lead to the outside world, such as a rural vista, or to another room in the house.

A louvred door creates a feeling of receding depth in a mural — the gaps between the slats could offer glimpses of the scene beyond. Add Chromium Oxide Green to the red to create the deeper shadow tone. Use Cadmium Yellow to lighten the Red, as White will tend to make the colour go pink.

An open window with a plain white frame will not interrupt the flow of the landscape beyond, as this will be visible through the glass. To divide the open window into four panes, draw two diagonal lines from corner to corner. Where the lines intersect is the middle of the window, so draw a vertical line at this point and use the vanishing point to draw the receding horizontal.

This design demonstrates clearly the use of one-point perspective. The horizon line of the sea
is the same as the eye-level line. The vanishing point is shown in the middle of this line.
Note how the receding lines of the floor tiles and the louvred doors all converge at this point.

This rustic window, above, opens on to a view of a vineyard in Tuscany, and a bottle and glass of red wine, from the Chianti region, sit on the windowsill to bring the theme into the foreground. Pages 50–51 show how to paint realistic glasses and bottles.

A simple piece of fabric draped over a curtain pole will soften the edges of an otherwise stark window frame (see page 49). The pot of flowers in the foreground brings the window to life, and provides opportunity for detail that looks so real it will keep the viewer guessing.

WHAT COULD be more relaxing than the view of fields, trees and distant hills? The ideas here bring a sense of space and light into any room of the house. You may want to embellish the window frames with ivy or rustic accessories (see the next few pages for ideas) depending on which room you have chosen.

For a garden scene with perspective, try a pergola surround, framing an archway cut in a hedge, leading to a vista further beyond. This is a simple way to create an interesting view-beyond-a-view.

Here is a twist on the trompe l'oeil window — you could almost peer through the window into a rustic cottage! This would be effective in a conservatory or other extension — the 'original' window appearing to still be intact. The glass of wine and napkin add depth to the windowsill.

A GRAPEVINE growing up the side of a wall and then along the top of an arch or doorway makes a fantastic framing element for a landscape mural, especially if the view includes a distant vineyard. Intertwine ivy with classical stonework (pages 64–73) for a soft, aged look; twist it through trellis in a kitchen or conservatory (see page 36) or use it as a backdrop for real plants to merge reality with illusion.

The vine leaf shape is easy to sketch. First, lightly draw a rough circle using a charcoal pencil, then sketch a line dividing the circle in two. From about a third of the way along this line, draw four slightly curved lines to form the structure or skeleton of the leaf. It is now a simple task to flesh out the leaf shape, adding the crinkly edges. This leaf is flat, but the basic technique can be adapted to draw the leaves at different angles. Build up the colour using Chromium Oxide Green, Leaf Green and White.

A trained ivy plant in a plain terracotta pot would make a simple feature in the foreground of a mural. A matching pair could perhaps be placed on either side of a doorway. Paint the basic shape of the twisting plant in Chromium Oxide Green using a 1.5mm (⁵⁄₈in) flat brush. , Mix a lighter green using Chromium Oxide Green, Leaf Green and White, and use a No. 3 round pointed brush to paint the lower edges of an individual leaf, then smudge the colour upward to blend into the deep green. Repeat this all over the plant, and add a few straggly leaves breaking away from the clipped shape. Mix some Paynes Grey into the Chromium Oxide Green to pick out some deeper shadows, especially on the side of the plant that is further from the light source — in this case, the left-hand side.

Ivy leaves can be planned out in a very similar way to the vine leaves opposite. In this case, the leaf is more pointed. Ivy leaves are quite dark: use Chromium Oxide Green with a little Paynes Grey. The veins and edges of the leaves have been picked out with White mixed with the leaf colour.

A SIMPLE arrangement of flowers, or even a single stem, makes an excellent foreground subject, for instance on a windowsill, when you are painting a country view, linking the painted frame with the landscape. You could also paint a vase of flowers on a real or trompe l'oeil shelf or table, such as those on the next few pages.

Use Permanent Rose for pink rose flowers, lightening the colour by adding White to pick out the upper surfaces of the petals. This will define the form of the flowers.

Outline a clear glass bottle in a mix of Paynes Grey and White, blended out toward the middle. Add a little of the background colour. The colour of the water is deepened at the top, to emphasize the contrast with the light reflected on its surface. The stem of the rose is also shown slightly refracted as it passes through the water surface. A subtle green wash glazed over the water area gives a slightly murky look.

These white daisies would also work very well if painted against a deep background colour to give a strong contrast. .

The part of the tulip I love the most is not the flower but the wonderfully expressive leaf, which unfurls from around the stem as it grows. The leaves here are a little more stylized than real. The flower is painted in Cadmium Orange and Cadmium Yellow, and gives a bold, contemporary feel suitable for a modern sitting room.

These geraniums have very rounded leaves: use a paler green to delineate their crisp edges and contrast with the deeper green veins, then blend it in toward the middle of each leaf. The flowers are simply painted as a cluster of blobs, using a mixture of Permanent Rose and White.

For a collection of china that is both
unbreakable and never requires dusting,
a row of willow pattern plates would be
ideal, mounted onto a real or trompe
l'oeil shelf.

Transfer the willow pattern design for
the plate on to the wall. Use Cobalt
Blue and White with Nos.1 and 3
round pointed brush to pick out the
details, although do not try to copy the
willow design to the exact last detail.

A lace effect is easy to achieve, and is a subtle way to enhance a bare
wall or plain shelf. Photocopy or scan a piece of lace and use this to
trace the design on to the wall. Paint in the design with Red Oxide
before painting on the background colours. Then use Nos.1 and 3
round point brushes to pick out the lace work with White paint.

EVEN THE simplest of embellishments can add country charm to a kitchen or dining room. Create a collection of teapots by experimenting with different colours and patterns. For a believable effect, everything in the collection should be lit from the same direction. In addition, a stark kitchen window that has only a blind would benefit from a pair of checked curtains to soften the window frame and add colour and movement.

The use of a pattern on fabric helps to suggest form through the folding and bunching, as seen with the blue and white checked curtain opposite. In the case of the red and white curtain (right), the pattern has been used to suggest movement as it blows in the breeze from an open window. To re-create this effect, first block the curtain in with base colour, in this case an off white, then build up highlights and shadows to suggest folds. Very lightly plan out the pattern on the curtain using a charcoal pencil — note how the pattern follows the shape at the bottom of the curtain. Finally, use a suitable round or flat brush to paint in the design using a deeper shade to suggest the folds and shadow.

Highlights and shadow suggest the smooth curves of an object, such as this teapot. A touch of highlight on the spout, lid and handle bring the surface to life, while the highlight on the body of the teapot suggests a reflected window.

A HALF-FILLED glass of wine and a half empty bottle provide a relaxed focal point in a mural, and are simple to add to a window sill or table. Why not paint them on a dining room sideboard, or on the wall at the back of the kitchen work surface?

The wine bottle is built up with a mixture of Leaf Green, Chromium Oxide Green and White — the highlights emphasize the curvature of the bottle. The red wine colour is a mixture of Red Oxide and Chromium Oxide Green, which deepens the red for the shading.

For the edges of the glass use Paynes Grey, Raw Umber and White with Nos. 1 and 3 round pointed brushes. Note the white highlights, the way the wine colour is reflected down the stem of the glass and the colours of the tablecloth, visible through the base of the glasses.

The champagne bottle uses the same greens as the wine bottle, but add some Paynes Grey to the mix for the deep tones along the edges, to accentuate the curvature. Yellow Ochre, Raw Umber and White have been stippled on for the gold coloured foil. Simply suggest the lettering on the label, and turn the bottle so the label is off-centre and partly obscured.

Use Raw Sienna mixed with White for the champagne in these flute glasses — add a little Raw Umber to blend in a deeper tone around the edges. Dab on some bubbles with White and a No. 3 round pointed brush, and repeat for the fizzing along the surface of the champagne.

THE CONTENTS of a
country kitchen offer lots
of potential to enhance your mural
with extra details, such as a notice
board with postcards, cookery books,
utensils and cooking ingredients on
kitchen shelves. Why not paint the
doors of plain kitchen cupboards
to give the illusion that they are
stocked with homemade preserves
or pots and pans?

Various interesting wall surfaces are shown here, including a crumbling brick wall, cracked plaster, and tongue-and-groove panelling. The bunch of lavender would also look effective hanging from a window frame or shutter framing a rustic landscape.

Wherever possible, use the real objects for reference. Use different textures to create visual interest: here the sharp reflective highlights on the bottles and grater contrast with the subtle shading on the eggs and terracotta jar.

Classical Details

The architecture of classical Greece left an
enduring legacy, which can still be seen in
building styles today. The classical orders were
embraced by the Romans, who built upon the
beauties of Greek architecture by introducing
rounded arches in their desire to build on a
larger scale. Their influence spread throughout
the western world with the growth of the
Roman empire, and the architects of the
Renaissance returned to the grace and
proportions of classical style, which could still
be seen in the buildings that had survived since
ancient times. It remains an essential part of
the fabric of our modern environment,
forming an architectural link with a culture
of 2,500 years ago.

The decorative details of 18th- and 19th-
century homes, which we love today for the
charm and elegance they add to period
interiors, often drew on classical conventions.
Trompe l'oeil techniques allow you to add
architectural distinction of this kind to a plain
interior, by creating the illusion of carved
pediments above doorways, or by adding
pillars, panelling and mouldings. You can also
incorporate classical details in a painted vista,
such as a balustrade to frame the view, or a
crumbling ruin in the distance.

Stone Rosette Panel

THIS IS A SIMPLE architectural ornament that could be used effectively as a detail in a larger scheme incorporating decorative stonework, or to enhance a trompe l'oeil architectural feature such as a decorative door frame or faux panelling. In a large-scale project this kind of motif might be repeated, but a single rosette would make an attractive decoration for a chimney piece, a cupboard door or perhaps a plinth supporting an urn – either real or painted in a mural. Pages 64–67 show further intricate stonework features that could be isolated and used as embellishments in the same way.

The three-dimensional form is quickly achieved by adding shadow and highlight tones to the simple design, and you can apply this technique to almost any carved shape. Since the relief effect depends entirely on light and shade, it's important to establish the direction of the light source, and this must be consistent if you are painting more than one motif. In this example, the light is coming from the upper left, so the shadows are cast down to the right. Keep standing back to view the effect – you will soon see if it is working.

Stone Rosette Panel 57

Palette

White

Flesh Tint

Cobalt Blue

Naples Yellow

1 Trace and scale up the rosette on transfer paper. The example shown here is 16cm (6½in) in diameter. Decide on the position for the centre of the motif on the wall, and use a spirit level and charcoal pencil to draw horizontal and vertical guidelines intersecting at this point. Draw guidelines on the design to help you line it up, and transfer the design to the wall.

2 Remove the transfer paper, and use compasses to draw in the circle around the design (stick some masking tape over the centre point to protect the wall, and to stop the compasses from slipping).

3 Ensuring that the rosette is centrally placed, lightly draw the lines for the square panel using a spirit level and charcoal pencil. In this example the inner panel is 40cm (15½in) wide and the outer panel is 46cm (18in). Mix some Flesh Tint, Cobalt Blue and a little White with a small amount of water. Use a No. 3 round pointed brush to paint over all the outlines, using a straight edge for the panel lines.

4 Mix three light colours for the stone, using White and Naples Yellow, White and Flesh Tint, and White and Cobalt Blue. Mix 1–2 parts water into each colour. Using a 25mm (1in) hog-hair brush, paint over the whole design, building up a subtle stone effect by alternating between the three colours (use the White and Naples Yellow colour sparingly). You should still be able to see the outlines. Use the brush in all directions and stipple the colour in places, perhaps adding a little white if it is getting too dark.

5 The outline colour mixed in step 3 can be used as a shadow tone. Using Nos. 3 and 5 round pointed brushes, pick out the shadows cast by the relief carving, using the colours from step 4 to soften the shadow edges. As you paint the shadow around the circular base, gradually increase the pressure to thicken the line, then decrease to taper it. Paint a crescent-shaped shadow on the centre on the rosette, then blend the colour toward the other side. Because the square panel is recessed, the top and left-hand edges are painted in the shadow tone.

6 Highlight the edges catching the light, in this case the top left edges all around the moulding, using White and a No. 3 round pointed brush. Again use the colours from step 4 to blend it down. Highlight the bottom and right-hand side of the panel, using a straight edge if necessary.

7 Use the colours from step 4 with a 15mm (⁵⁄₈in) flat brush to deepen the stone colour adjacent to the highlights. This will provide a bolder contrast to emphasize the highlights. Blend in a little of the shadow colour from step 5 as well if necessary.

8 To add a subtle texture to the stone effect, dip the bristles of an old toothbrush into a little of the outline colour from step 3. Spatter the paint at random on to the wall, using your thumb to flick the bristles. Vary the distance between the brush and the wall for slightly different effects.

Stone Rosette Panel 59

Doorway Pediment

IF YOU WANT TO ADD an architectural flourish to a plain door, a trompe l'oeil pediment painted above it can dramatically enhance its appearance, providing a grand entrance to the room beyond.

When designing a pediment to fit the top of your doorway, you need to ensure that the pitch you use suits the space available between the top of the architrave and the ceiling. The pitch will probably need to be lower if you are planning a pediment over a double door. Remember that you need only scale up half the pediment on transfer paper, as it is symmetrical.

The pediment could be painted on its own, on a plain or colourwashed wall, or could form part of a larger trompe l'oeil scheme, incorporating other architectural features such as stone blocking, balustrading and columns, perhaps with views over an Arcadian landscape. Pages 64–73 offer plenty of ideas that will allow you to bring a classical feel to any room of the house.

Palette

Raw Umber

White

Flesh Tint

Windsor Violet

Paynes Grey

1 The diagram above includes the design for the pediment described in this project (left) as well as a simplified version (right). You will need to adjust the design to fit your doorway, before scaling up one half of the pediment on to transfer paper.

2 Measure the top of the doorway to find the centre, and draw a faint vertical line from it using a spirit level and charcoal pencil. Position the scaled-up drawing on the wall so it lines up with the top edge of the architrave and the centre vertical. Transfer only the outline of the image to the wall, then flip the paper and repeat for the other half of the pediment. Remove the drawing and retain for later.

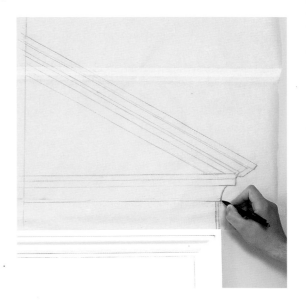

3 Using White thinned with a little water and a 15mm (5/8in) flat brush, carefully cut in the line of the pediment around the edges. (You may wish to use low-tack masking tape to achieve crisper edges.) Use a larger decorator's brush to fill in the middle, and repeat until you have a reasonably even covering.

4 Mix three subtle colours: White with a small amount of Paynes Grey, White with Flesh Tint, and White with Flesh Tint and a small amount of Paynes Grey. Add a little water to each colour. Using a 25mm (1in) hog-hair brush, stipple the colours over the pediment to create a subtle pinky/grey stone effect. Repeat if necessary, then leave to dry. Position the transfer paper again, and trace off all the pediment detail for both sides.

5 Add a little more Paynes Grey and Flesh Tint to the colours mixed in step 4, to create a shadow tone. Pick out the detail and shadows using a No. 7 round pointed brush. Use a spirit level as a guide to keep the lines straight. If the light source is above right, the cast shadows will be more pronounced on the right-hand side.

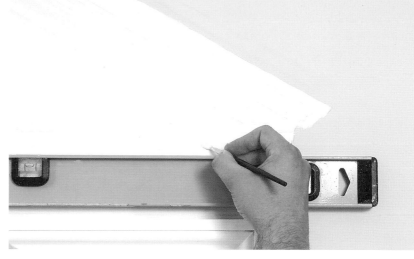

6 Mix a darker shadow tone and use Nos. 3 and 5 round pointed brushes to pick out the deeper shadows on the underside of the mouldings. Do not paint the cast shadows in this darker tone. Paint the highlights on the pediment in white – especially along the top edge of the moulding forming the bottom of the triangle.

7 Using a 15mm (⁵/₈in) flat brush, blend White thinned with a little water over the pediment near the cast shadows (do not paint over the shadows). This will sharpen the contrast at the edge of the shadow. You can also use a stone colour slightly darker than those used in step 4 to deepen the pediment colour next to a highlight, making the highlight more prominent.

8 Mix the colour for the shadow cast on the wall. In this example, a little Raw Umber, Paynes Grey and Windsor Violet were added to the yellow emulsion (latex) paint. Using a 15mm (⁵/₈in) flat brush, paint a cast shadow to the lower left of the pediment, roughly copying the shape of the pediment edge. You may need to use some of the original wall colour to sharpen the edge of the shadow.

COLUMNS ARE very versatile when used in a trompe l'oeil scene. They can be part of the landscape, or may be used as architectural elements flanking a view. Use the examples on these pages, which show the various decorative orders introduced by the Greeks, scaling them up to fit your measurements. Establish the centre vertical on the wall before lightly marking in the outlines. The column shaft should be slightly wider at the bottom than at the top. It may be helpful to fix two lengths of string on the wall (held with masking tape) to represent the sides of the column before you start drawing, to give you an idea of the effect.

The Tuscan style has no ornament and would be ideal to try first. Note that the top and bottom of the shaft are curved where they meet the capital and base, to suggest the curvature of the column.

The Corinthian order has a capital richly decorated with acanthus leaves and scrolls, which is shown below in more detail. You could also decorate the plain shaft of the column with a marble effect.

The Doric order is the most massive of the four columns shown here. It has no base: the shaft sits directly on the platform. The shaft is grooved but, unlike the Ionic column, the grooves meet in a sharp ridge and are not separated by a flat band.

The Ionic order has a scroll-like capital and a tall shaft, with decorative fluting separated by flat bands, as can be seen in the detail below. When you are planning the fluting, ensure that the grooves appear closer together toward the edges to suggest the curvature of the column. The fluting can also be picked out with shadows and fine highlights.

AN URN on a pedestal can provide a central focal point for a trompe l'oeil scene – for instance, it might be viewed through a trellis archway and backed by a formal garden. You can also inject extra colour and interest by filling it with flowers or foliage (see opposite). Use the ivy shown on page 45 to soften the stonework, trailing it over the edges of the pot, or creeping around the base.

These designs for urns and plinths can be scaled up to suit your needs. You need only trace and enlarge half of each design, because they are symmetrical. Flip the tracing paper over to transfer the opposite side of the design.

Pay careful attention to the light source when depicting the decorative mouldings. You should mix at least three stone colours: a base colour (mid-tone), a shadow tone and a light tone, although I recommend using more variations. The Stone Rosette Panel project gives an example of a stone colour mixed using Flesh Tint, Cobalt Blue, Naples Yellow and White.

The shading on the urn is subdued, suggesting the rounded stone surface, while the highlights and shading on the pedestal are much sharper, to help emphasize its angular form.

ELEGANCE, BALANCE and rhythm are important in a classical mural, and balustrading adds all three. Balustrades can be used as an attractive yet subtle boundary. Painted in the foreground of a mural, they create a sense of perspective without dominating the overall scene.

If you are using a row of balusters as the foreground to a trompe l'oeil view, they should be scaled up to a height of about 60cm (24in), with a rail along the top about 9cm (3½in) deep, and a plinth about 11.5cm (4½in) high. I usually space balusters so that the gaps between them are about a half to three-quarters of the width of the base.

Combining a row of balustrading with an obelisk, or an urn set on a plinth can be very effective. This kind of feature can be the main focus in the middle of a mural, or a pair could frame a view into a classical garden.

Because the balusters are rounded they look the same seen from the front, to the left or the right. However, the tops and bases are angular and there will be variations as you look down a row of balustrading, because you will begin to see the sides as well as the front faces. An understanding of one-point perspective can help here. Because there is no ornament on the bulbous part of the baluster it is important to use light and shade to define the form. In these examples the light is coming from the upper right, so the colour deepens toward the bottom left. The colour lightens slightly along the left edge as this will be picking up reflected light bouncing off other objects.

An alternative to balustrading is a parapet wall with a decorative screen. Architectural features like these are effective in dividing the background from the foreground without interfering too much with the view (see page 54). Glimpses of the landscape through balustrades and pierced walls contrast effectively with the stonework, emphasizing its shape.

AN ARCHITRAVE across the top of a mural completes the classical framework provided by a pair of columns. Architraves such as those shown here would make an impressive fireplace surround, emulating the stone surrounds that have been popular throughout the centuries. A decorative architrave would also create a beautiful headboard for a bed, intertwined with flowers and foliage for a soft, romantic feel.

Add interest with a decorative frieze, such as the rows of small blocks, called dentils, shown above.

This is a very simple pediment to plan and paint, and would be suitable in a situation where there is not much clearance above the door. The keystone in the centre protrudes slightly, and thus casts a shadow.

To plan a segmental pediment, use a pencil and a piece of string. The lower down the doorway you place the fulcrum for the curve, the shallower the arch will be.

The simple fluted design of this
frieze is similar to that used for the
shaft of an Ionic column (page 65).

There are many possible variations of the Doorway Pediment project on
pages 60—63, using the same planning and painting techniques. You could
even add quirky details like a perched bird or a butterfly to the design —
the injection of colour against the stonework would contrast well. Remember
that the amount of space between the top of the doorway and the ceiling will
dictate the kind of design you are able to paint.

This design is known as a broken pediment
and is similar to that used in the Doorway
Pediment project (pages 60—63), except that
a circular break has been cut out of the top.

This pediment was inspired by the Wisteria
Trellis project (pages 36—39). A little
trailing greenery could be added to complete
the rustic effect.

THE DEPICTION of classical ruins was a popular romantic theme. The fact that ancient monuments, built to impose order on the landscape, were ultimately succumbing to nature held great appeal – and still does. A crumbling ruin, overgrown with moss and ivy, against an Arcadian backdrop, provides a expressive and magical link with the past. The ruin could be part of a classical scene, the focal point of a landscape, or a folly conceived as a decorative feature of a romantic garden.

Ruins can be fun to paint but be careful not to overdo it — the brush is a powerful tool and your once magnificent temple could be reduced to a pile of rubble in a few strokes. To paint cracks, first paint and smudge in the direction of the crack in a deep tone, then add a finer line using a No. 1 or 3 round pointed brush and a very deep tone. Highlights can be added corresponding to the light source. Experiment and keep the painting fluid and random, to help the effect look more natural.

The Water's Edge

For mural painters, the theme of water is an almost limitless resource for inspiration, from waterfalls and raging rapids, to serene lakes reflecting distant mountains; from rivers meandering through the countryside, to waves breaking on a tropical shore; from ships sailing across vast oceans to the mysteries of the deep ocean – and it is said that we know more about the surface of the moon than we do about our oceans and the life contained there.

Water is a vital element for the survival of all plants and animals, but it is not only essential to our physical wellbeing. The sight of a sparkling stream raises the spirits, while gazing over a sheet of placid water with its rippling reflections induces a deep sense of calm.

A mural with a watery theme can help to instil that same sense of peace in your home. It is an ideal subject for an area where you relax, such as a sitting room or a bathroom, where a vista of golden sand lapped by gentle waves will transport you far from mundane chores and chilly weather.

Seagull and Lighthouse

THE SEA HAS BEEN AN INSPIRATION for many artists – most notably J. M. W. Turner, whose fantastical stormy seascapes captured the sheer ferocity of crashing waves and heaving seas. This mural opts for a calmer approach, with gentle waves lapping on the sandy shore and a seagull stopping for a rest in the salty breeze. The lighthouse is a reassuring element, in case the calm weather takes a turn for the worse.

The colours – cool blues, greys and greens – are subtle and harmonious. The red lighthouse, in sharp contrast, provides visual interest, and the seagull in the foreground appears to be looking back at the lighthouse, forming a link between the two. The subdued colours sit well with the faded driftwood frame, bound with rope.

This mural on a marine theme (see the Design Library for more ideas) would work well in a bathroom, or even in a bedroom, where the emphasis is on relaxation. As it is painted on a board, it can be moved into its final position after completion, but remember to note where the light source will ultimately be, so you can relate it to the painting.

Palette

Red Oxide

Raw Umber

White

Burnt Sienna

Cadmium Yellow

Windsor Violet

Cobalt Blue

Coeruleum Blue

Chromium
Oxide Green

Paynes Grey

Phthalo Turquoise

Black

Flesh Tint

Cadmium Orange

Naples Yellow

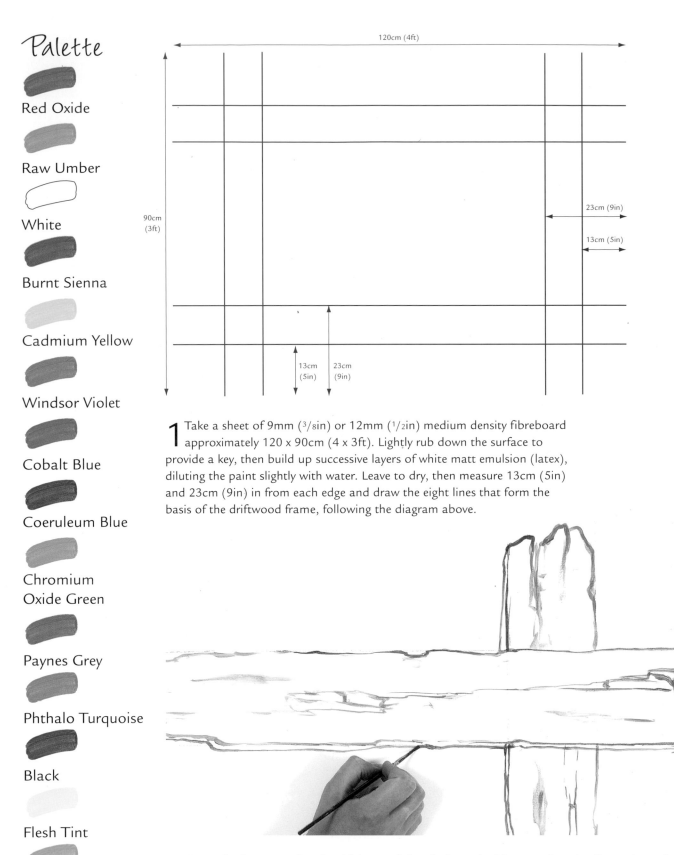

120cm (4ft)

90cm
(3ft)

23cm (9in)

13cm (5in)

13cm
(5in)

23cm
(9in)

1 Take a sheet of 9mm ($^3/_8$in) or 12mm ($^1/_2$in) medium density fibreboard approximately 120 x 90cm (4 x 3ft). Lightly rub down the surface to provide a key, then build up successive layers of white matt emulsion (latex), diluting the paint slightly with water. Leave to dry, then measure 13cm (5in) and 23cm (9in) in from each edge and draw the eight lines that form the basis of the driftwood frame, following the diagram above.

2 Draw the frame, varying the thickness of the planks and adding weathered splits to the ends. Plan this first using a charcoal pencil, or go straight into Red Oxide paint with a No. 3 or No. 5 round pointed brush: the latter will give a more fluid line. Do not use a straight edge, as the lines need to look soft and weathered. Suggest splitting and pits, using your fingers to smudge the line in places. Note that the horizontal planks overlay the vertical planks. Add another line about 6mm ($^1/_4$in) in from each inside edge, to suggest the thickness of the wood.

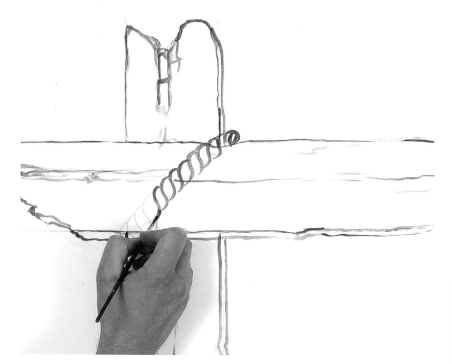

3 Sketch in the ropes at the corners using simple repeated S-shaped strokes. One diagonal rope binds each corner of the frame. The top left rope goes diagonally up from left to right, and the top right rope goes diagonally down from left to right. The ropes in the lower corners should mirror those in the top corners.

4 Wearing a protective mask to avoid inhaling sawdust, cut around the outer edge of the frame using a jigsaw. Sand all the cut edges thoroughly, smoothing over the corners, then paint them as in step 1. Drill a hole in each corner to take suitable fixings, positioning them to give the impression that they are holding the planks together: do not put the fixings through the ropes as this will spoil the illusion. Attach the panel to a wall.

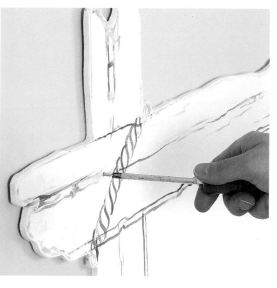

5 Tape transfer paper to the panel and plan the landscape. Sketch in the horizon line about 29cm (11¹/₂in) from the bottom of the panel. Draw the lighthouse, cliff and sea wall. The horizon line cuts though the lower half of the house, and the wall sits below the horizon. Suggest the water curving along to the left of the panel and the distant hills. When you are happy with the design, transfer it to the panel and paint in the outlines using Red Oxide and a No. 3 round pointed brush.

6 Attach another sheet of transfer paper and sketch the seagull and its perch, using photographic references if you wish. Transfer the design to the wall and outline in Red Oxide.

7 Mix up a wash using White, Raw Umber and Naples Yellow with 3–4 parts water. Using a 25mm (1in) hog-hair brush, wash the colour over the whole panel. When painting the driftwood frame, keep the brush strokes in the direction of the grain. Leave to dry and repeat.

8 Mix a similar colour to the wash, adding only a little water and mixing in more Raw Umber and a little Cobalt Blue. Using a 15mm (5/8in) flat brush, loosely paint in some of the grain and splitting detail along each plank. Vary the angle of the brush to open and close the splits and gaps. Add some cast shadows on the vertical planks where the horizontal planks cross them, and add the small shadows cast by the ropes. The light in this case is coming from the top left.

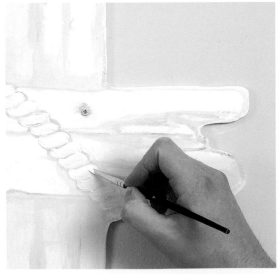

9 Mix White with a little Raw Umber. Using a No. 7 round pointed brush paint the rope, following the S-shape and applying more pressure to the middle of the brush stroke so the line thickens and then tapers. Mix some more Raw Umber into the paint to pick out the deeper shadows in the twists of the rope.

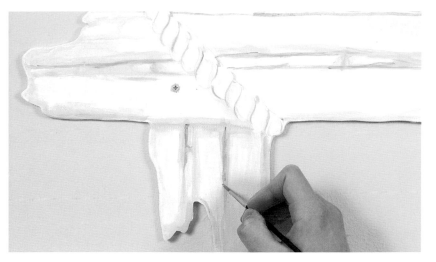

10 Add more Raw Umber and a little more Cobalt Blue to some of the colour mixed in step 8. Using Nos. 1 and 3 round pointed brushes, pick out the finer, deeper shadows in the wood splits. Also use some of the original colour from step 8, blending and smudging with your fingers to achieve the desired effect.

11 Mix a colour similar to the wash used in step 7, adding more White and only a little water. Use a 15mm (⁵⁄₈in) flat brush to pick out some of the highlights along the tops of the planks and the wood splits. Where there is a horizontal split in the wood, the area immediately below is highlighted; along the vertical splits the highlight is to the right.

12 Mix three gentle shades of sky blue using White, Coeruleum Blue and Cobalt Blue, adding a little water to each. Paint the sky with a 15mm (⁵⁄₈in) flat brush, starting with the deepest blue at the top and gradually blending down to a very pale blue on the horizon. Add a small amount of Burnt Sienna to some of the deepest blue, and block in the distant hills. Start building up the shadow tones on the seagull using some of the colours used for the frame.

13 Using the lightest blue and a 15mm (⁵⁄₈in) flat brush, build up some loose clouds behind the lighthouse and thinner ones along the horizon. Use a little water on the brush to blend the bottom of the clouds, and a little white to pick out highlights on the tops. Mix White with a little Windsor Violet and 2 parts water to add purple shadows to the bottom of the clouds, again using a little water on the brush to stop the colours becoming too defined.

14 Mix White, Chromium Oxide Green and Cobalt Blue with a little water. Using a 10mm (³/₈in) flat brush, stipple in some foliage behind the lighthouse, tapering it out along the coastline to the left. Mix a slightly deeper shade by adding more Chromium Oxide Green and Cobalt Blue, and stipple along the bottom of the foliage, blending it into the lighter colour.

15 Mix four colours for the sea and sand, adding a little water to each: 1. White and Cobalt Blue, to a slightly deeper shade than the deepest sky colour; 2. White, Cobalt Blue and Phthalo Turquoise; 3. White, Naples Yellow and Raw Umber; 4. White and Naples Yellow. Starting at the horizon and using a 15mm (⁵/₈in) flat brush with colour 1, paint with horizontal strokes, blending the paint down into colour 2 and then into colour 3 where the waves break, then into colour 4 up to the edge of the frame. Repeat until there is a reasonably smooth transition of colour. Paint a thin strip of colour 4 under the distant foliage to look like a faraway beach, tapering the colour out to the left.

16 Add a little water to some White and with a 10mm (³/₈in) flat brush, loosely paint some gentle lapping waves along the area where colours 2 and 3 blend together. Use slightly curved horizontal strokes, with a little water on the brush to blend out the top of the wave, keeping the bottom edge defined. Do not overdo this – the trick is to keep it simple. Using colour 4 mixed in step 15, add a fine cast shadow under the lapping waves in the foreground.

17 Start blocking in the lighthouse using Cadmium Orange and Red Oxide. For the house, use White and a mix of White with a little Paynes Grey and Flesh Tint. Note that the right-hand side of the house is in shadow. Use this shadow colour for the right-hand side of the white bands of the lighthouse. Add a little Chromium Oxide Green to the lighthouse red for the shading on the red bands. Using a No. 6 flat brush, pick out the the detailing on the windows and doors with the grey shade, adding a little more Paynes Grey if necessary. Mix some White, Burnt Sienna and Raw Umber for the roof. Use the driftwood frame colours to block in the sea wall. For the grass on the clifftop, mix some Chromium Oxide Green into some of the sand colour 4 mixed in Step 15. Block in the colour using a 15mm (⁵/₈in) flat brush.

18 Pick out the fine detailing on the sea wall with a No. 1 round pointed brush, using the deepest frame colour mixed in step 10. Loosely suggest pebbles on the beach, using your finger to smudge the line of the reflection in the water. Build up the colours on the lighthouse, mixing Chromium Oxide Green into some of the red to add a shadow down the right-hand side. Pick out the railings with a No. 3 round pointed brush, highlighting with a little White. Add window shutters to the house using the roof colour mixed in step 17 and a No. 6 flat brush.

19 Mix a warm light grey using White, Flesh Tint and a little Paynes Grey with a little water, and block in the seagull's wings using a 15mm (⁵/₈in) flat brush and a No. 10 flat brush. For the seagull's breast, mix White with a little Flesh Tint. Blend in some of the wing colour to shade under the head and beak, and where the legs join. Add a little more Paynes Grey to some of the wing colour and pick out the deeper colour on the tail. Mix some White, Flesh Tint and Cadmium Yellow, and paint the legs and beak with Nos. 1 and 3 round pointed brushes.

20 Using a No. 1 round pointed brush, or finer, pick out the final details on the seagull. Deepen the shadow above the eye and under the beak. Colour the eye with White and Cadmium Yellow, using a few coats to build up a vibrant colour. Once dry, add a small pupil with Black and, when this has dried, add a small blob of white to the top left of the pupil so that it overlaps the yellow. This simple highlight has the effect of bringing the eye to life. Pick out some of the feathers to suggest the plumage, using a slightly deeper grey than that used to paint the wings and some White. Use White to pick out some of the feather tips – especially along the tail. Use some of the deeper grey to give more definition to the details on the beak.

Fish Mosaic

Mosaic is an ancient and enduring method of creating pictures or abstract designs by embedding tiny pieces of stone or marble, called 'tesserae', in cement. The Romans, who learnt the skill from the ancient Greeks, created designs of great subtlety using stone and coloured glass cut into small squares.

Viewed from a distance, a mosaic may itself be a trompe l'oeil, and the illusion is doubled when the little coloured squares are in fact painted on a flat surface. The subtle variations of colour and texture that characterize mosaics give them great visual appeal, and this quality is easy to replicate in paint. The painted mosaic can be given an aged effect, as here, by leaving a few pieces missing from the design.

This simple fish design could be developed into a frieze, using it as a repeating motif or adding different fish and sea shells. Both the marine theme (extended in the Design Library pages) and the mosaic style would be appropriate for a bathroom, or even for a kitchen, where the fish could be accompanied by lobsters, crabs and other seafood.

Fish Mosaic 85

Palette

Raw Umber

White

Flesh Tint

Naples Yellow

Cobalt Blue

Coeruleum Blue

Burnt Sienna

Paynes Grey

1 The mosaic design is applied using square stamps, which can be cut from high density foam (such as upholstery foam) using a craft knife. The decorative checkerboard stamp shown here was found in a craft shop and simply cut into separate squares. Mix the paint on a plate to make it easy to pick up on the stamps.

2 Mix a warm grey base colour using White, Naples Yellow, a little Raw Umber and a little Paynes Grey. You will need enough for at least two coats, plus some spare for touching up later. Paint the wall and leave to dry, then lightly draw a horizontal guideline using a spirit level and charcoal pencil. Scale up the outline of the fish on the previous page on to transfer paper and trace it on to the wall. This fish is 59cm (23in) long, and the stamps are 14mm (¹/₂in) square.

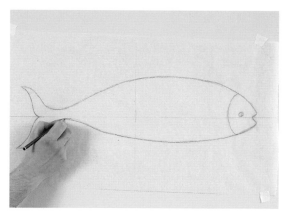

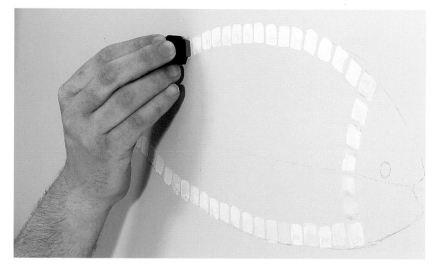

3 Mix White with Naples Yellow and use to stamp the outline of the fish, being careful not to overload the stamp with paint. Leave a small gap between each square, and keep the squares to the inside of the outline. The squares will overlap in places – especially when you are painting the tail – but you can use some of the base colour later to redefine the mosaic pieces. Instead of stamping very small pieces, such as the pointed end of the tail, paint them in with a No. 1 or 3 round pointed brush.

4 For the body of the fish mix Flesh Tint, Burnt Sienna and White. Starting around the edges, keep the mosaic rows following the arched shape of the fish. You can print small pieces by using only part of the stamp if you wish, or use a paint brush. Mix two shades of blue using White and Cobalt Blue, and White and Coeruleum Blue. Outline the fish, alternating the blues here and there for variation.

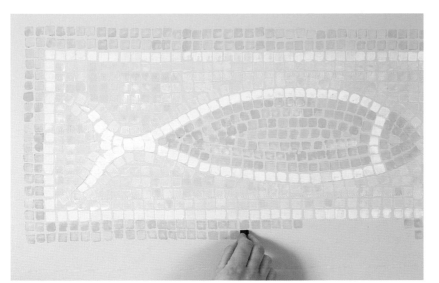

5 Lightly sketch in horizontal and vertical guidelines around the fish, using a charcoal pencil and a spirit level. Build up the blue area by stamping horizontal rows of squares, up to and in places overlapping the blue outline painted in step 4. The rows should be reasonably straight, but slight variations of level add to the attraction of this design. Add a simple border design using the colours used in steps 3 and 4.

6 Using Nos. 1 and 3 round pointed brushes and the original base colour, tidy up the tile edges where necessary. Where the stamps have overlapped, divide them up by painting a line through the middle to give some tiles irregular shapes.

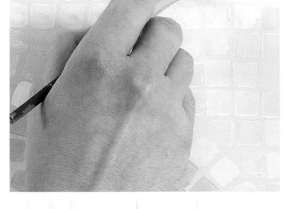

7 Using the base colour and a No. 10 flat brush, block out one or two of the mosaic squares in random areas, to suggest that the pieces have fallen away. Be careful not to overdo this.

8 Mix in a little more Raw Umber and Paynes Grey with the base colour. Using a No. 1 round pointed brush, pick out fine shadows along the bottom and right edges of some of the squares. Use your finger to smudge the shadow in places – smudging the colour over some of the squares can help the aged effect. Make some shadows thicker than others and leave some squares with no shadow, to give the impression that the surface is slightly uneven. You can also add highlights to the top and left edges of a few tiles using the tile colour mixed with a little more White, but don't overdo this.

Fish Mosaic 87

WHAT COULD be more relaxing then a white sandy beach, the sound of the sea lapping at the shore and palm trees swaying in the breeze? Recreate your favourite holiday memories in any room where you like to unwind. This complete scene would look stunning along the wall of a bedroom, allowing you to wake to a tropical beach scene every day. For a children's room, the sandcastle, bucket and spade from page 91 could be incorporated. The palm trees themselves would add a touch of dramatic greenery to a bathroom.

A tropical beach scene can be framed with palms and other exotic plants. On the horizon, add simple palm trees with a No. 1 or 3 round pointed brush, using some of the sea and sky blues mixed with a little Chromium Oxide Green. When building up a lot of foreground foliage, mix a darker green using Chromium Oxide Green and a little Paynes Grey. Use this dark tone to paint around the profile of the leaves, to make them stand out and give the foliage more depth.

When painting palm leaves try not to be too fussy. Lightly sketch in the spine of the leaf, curving downwards, then paint the fronds using a 15mm (⁵/₈in) flat brush. Work from the spine outward in bold strokes, tapering off at the ends. Use Chromium Oxide Green, and Chromium Oxide Green mixed with Cadmium Yellow for the deeper greens (darkening the colour near the spine by adding a little Paynes Grey). For the lighter greens use Leaf Green, and Leaf Green mixed with White. Use a finer round brush to paint in the sharp ends of each frond. Add a mix of Yellow Ochre and White to the leaf in places, to vary the colour.

This simple sea shell effect on a piece of driftwood could be used with the Seagull and Lighthouse project (pages 76–83).

The base colour for the starfish shape is a mixture of Burnt Umber, White and a little Cadmium Orange. The details have been picked out with Nos. 1 and 3 round pointed brushes, using Burnt Umber and Raw Umber, and the highlights are White with a little Burnt Umber.

I have kept the colours of the shells very faded and washed out, concentrating on their form.

A SANDCASTLE or two can add foreground interest to a mural on a seaside theme, leading your eye toward the beach beyond. The sandcastles could also be decorated with sea shells, like those shown opposite. This subject is a natural and popular choice for the bathroom, and a collection of sea shells, driftwood and starfish would add a sophisticated beach atmosphere.

To create sandcastles, use Raw Sienna and White for the basic sand colour, mixing in some Raw Umber for the shading. Use White mixed with a little Raw Sienna for the highlights. To get the sand effect, stipple the paint on with a 25mm (1in) hog-hair brush, using a 15mm (⁵/₈in) flat brush to stipple along the edges. You can also vary the texture by using a toothbrush to spatter the paint, as described in the Stone Rosette Panel project.

TROPICAL FISH are some of the most eyecatching animals in the world, and this amazing tropical scene would add a splash of colour to any room of the house. It could be the aquarium you have always longed for, or you may want to gaze at the exotic fish as you laze in the bath. Children are enchanted by underwater scenes, and would welcome a friendly dolphin on their bedroom wall.

For the background to an underwater scene, blend White at the top into a mix of White, Cobalt Blue and Coeruleum Blue. The sunken ship and distant coral are painted using two mixes of Cobalt Blue, White and a little Burnt Sienna. These deep blues help to push the ship and coral into the distance.

The dolphin is painted using the same colours as the ship and distant coral, again helping to push it further into the distance.

Sketch in the shapes of the foreground coral very lightly before painting the forms freehand in bright colours, which contrast sharply with the deeper, cooler blues to enhance the feeling of depth. Use a 15mm (⅝in) flat brush and Nos. 3 and 5 round pointed brushes to paint in the various forms, using Cadmium Yellow, Orange and Red, White and Leaf Green.

Trace the outlines of the fish and fill in the shapes with two or three coats of White, to cover the deep blue background. When dry, trace on the final details and block in the colours with White mixed with Cobalt Blue, and Cadmium Yellow.

This porthole design
might be overwhelming on a large wall, but
would be suited to a small panel in a bathroom. You can
choose what to view though the porthole — the underwater scene
opposite would do extremely well, or you could paint a tropical island
view, giving the porthole a more luxurious appearance, as if it were on an
ocean liner. For a child's room, the porthole might be on a spaceship, with a view
of stars and planets (see pages 118–119).

Plan the porthole shape and lightly paint the outlines using
Paynes Grey and a No. 3 round pointed brush. The metallic
effect is created using Silver acrylic, stippled on with a 25mm
(1in) hog-hair brush to give a rough texture. Blend Paynes
Grey with Silver to bring out the shadows and finer
detailing, and White for the highlights.

A rust effect can be achieved using Raw Umber and Burnt
Sienna blended into the Silver. Use this sparingly and restrict it
to areas that would naturally be prone to rusting, such as under
the porthole and the numerous rivets.

THE REFLECTIVE quality of water immediately instils a sense of calm and peace into even the busiest of people, so these scenes will add serenity wherever you choose to paint them. You may like to dine looking out over the water to a classical urn or temple, by framing the scene with a window frame or louvred doors. The boat scene would appeal to a sailing fanatic, and look charming on a child's bedroom wall. Use reflections to suggest still or moving water – the boat's reflection is distorted and fragmented, suggesting the movement of the sea.

Notice how the relationship between the heights of the trees and the temple varies in the reflection, because the trees are further away. Measure the height of the object from its foot (making allowances if it is on a hill) then repeat this measurement immediately below it to find the extent of the reflected image.

The foliage effect is easily achieved by stippling with a 25mm (1in) hog-hair brush. First stipple the distant foliage with a mix of White, Chromium Oxide Green and a little Cobalt Blue. Block in the main area of the foliage arch with Chromium Oxide Green, stippling the edges. Block in the urn and plinth with white. Stipple the flowers in a range of colours. Finally, pick out the detailing on the urn and plinth using White mixed with Paynes Grey and Flesh Tint in various shades. Using Chromium Oxide Green and a little Paynes Grey, darken the area behind the urn to help define the edges.

Use the same colours for the reflection in the still water. Stipple the paint again but use another brush loaded with a little water to drag the colour down slightly while the paint is wet — have a cloth handy to catch any runs.

Design Library 95

Children's Worlds

Although trompe l'oeil often uses realistic scenes in its attempts to trick the eye, there is no need to restrict your mural painting to what is present in the physical world. You can delve into the limitless realms of fantasy, while still using your skills in conveying depth and solidity to create the illusion of a three-dimensional scene.

Children's rooms are obviously the prime location for murals of this kind, and most of the subjects in this chapter have been designed with children in mind. Large-scale murals can transform children's bedrooms into their own fantasy kingdoms, and the themes you choose will naturally depend on their own interests, from enchanted castles and fairyland scenes, to an adventure in space. For a nursery wall, there are also some bright, friendly toys.

Fantasy murals can enchant adults as well as children. The castle walls and turrets shown on the following pages could be adapted to decorate a dining room or hall in gothic style, while theatrical red curtains could create a dramatic bedroom setting.

Magic Castle Window

IF YOU ASK A CHILD what they would most like to see outside their bedroom window, a fire-breathing dragon could well be high on the list. If such mythical beasts do not frequent your neighbourhood, you can always paint one, complete with a stony castle window through which to view it safely. For a young alchemist, you can also provide the necessary basic equipment: a pestle and mortar, a bottle of magic potion and the obligatory book of spells.

This mural works well on its own, but you could go further, giving the whole room a mythical medieval theme, with crumbling castle walls, turrets, battlements, drawbridges, hanging tapestries and jousting knights on horseback. The idea need not be restricted to decorating children's rooms – for a dining room with an ancestral feel, picture instead a castle window with a dramatic view across the calm waters of a lake, to dense forests and distant highlands. Use the stonework on pages 110–111 to create these amazing scenes.

Magic Castle Window 99

Palette

Red Oxide

Raw Umber

White

Flesh Tint

Burnt Sienna

Cadmium Yellow

Windor Violet

Raw Sienna

Cobalt Blue

Coeruleum Blue

Chromium Oxide Green

Paynes Grey

Yellow Naples

Cadmium Orange

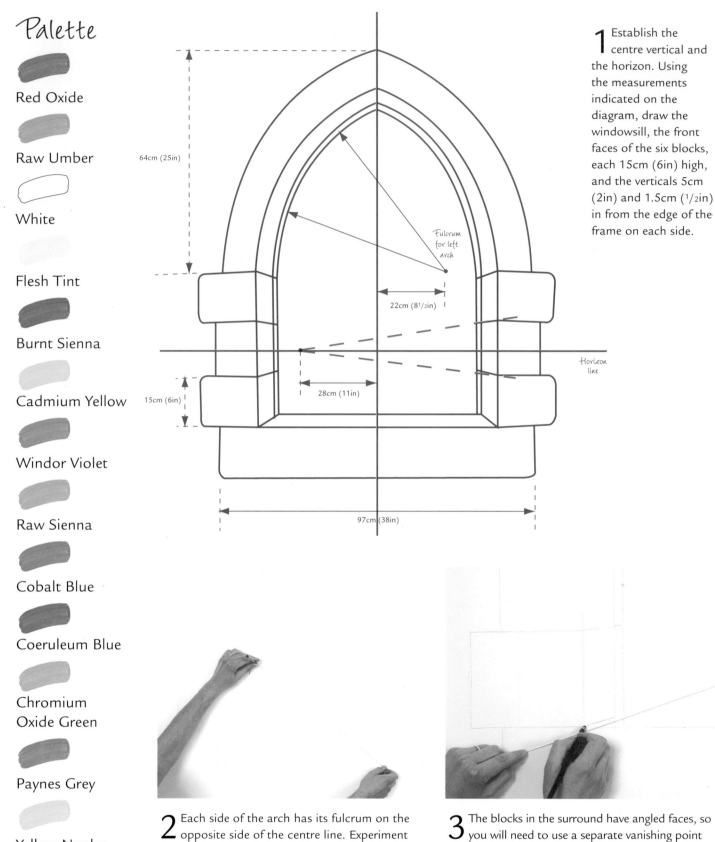

64cm (25in)

Fulcrum for left arch

22cm (8¹⁄₂in)

Horizon line

15cm (6in)

28cm (11in)

97cm (38in)

1 Establish the centre vertical and the horizon. Using the measurements indicated on the diagram, draw the windowsill, the front faces of the six blocks, each 15cm (6in) high, and the verticals 5cm (2in) and 1.5cm (¹⁄₂in) in from the edge of the frame on each side.

2 Each side of the arch has its fulcrum on the opposite side of the centre line. Experiment with different points to see the effect it has on the shape of the arch, but both fulcrums must be equidistant from the centre and at the same horizontal. Fix a length of string, with a pencil tied to the end, to each fulcrum to draw the curves.

3 The blocks in the surround have angled faces, so you will need to use a separate vanishing point for each side. Measure 28cm (11in) to either side of the centre along the horizon line. Use the vanishing point to the right to draw the receding lines of the blocks on the left, and the centre vanishing point to complete the lines of the inside return of the blocks. Repeat on the other side.

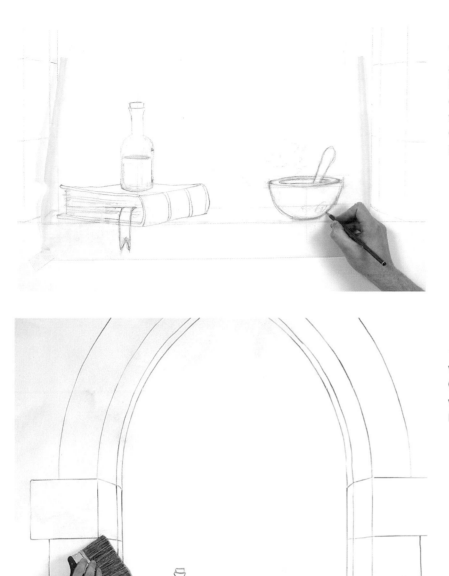

4 Fix transfer paper over the lower half of the window to plan the book, potion and pestle and mortar on the windowsill. To ensure the bottle and pestle are symmetrical, it may help to draw one half of each shape on a separate sheet, then fold it vertically to trace the second half. Once you are happy with the design, transfer it to the wall.

5 Paint over all the outlines in Red Oxide using a No. 3 round pointed brush. Mix up a wash with White, Naples Yellow and a little Paynes Grey, with about 4 parts water, and paint over the whole design using a large decorator's brush. Repeat when dry. The outlines will remain visible.

6 Mix up four stone colours, adding a very small amount of water to each but keeping the paint reasonably thick: White, Flesh Tint and Raw Umber; White, Flesh Tint and a little Paynes Grey; White, Burnt Sienna and a little Paynes Grey; White, Raw Sienna and a little Paynes Grey. Using a 15mm (5/8in) flat brush, cut in around the edge of the window surround, alternating between the different colours. Paint the rest of the area liberally using a 25mm (1in) hog-hair brush, blending the colours in and out of each other. Dab and roll a scrunched-up plastic bag over the wet paint to create a rough stony texture.

7 Mix a mortar colour using White and a little Raw Umber, adding a little water. Using a No. 10 flat brush, paint in the mortar lines, keeping the block sizes irregular. Start around the arch area, siting the stones so that they follow the arch shape, and then work outward. You may wish to sketch the mortar lines first with a light charcoal pencil before painting them. At least two coats will be needed as you are painting a lighter colour over a darker colour. Don't worry about neat, even lines or crisp edges, as you want to achieve a rough look. Touch in some of the stones with the colours from step 5 to vary their colours.

8 Mix White, Naples Yellow and a little Paynes Grey to give the same stone colour used for the wash, but of a much thicker consistency. Mix some of this colour with more Paynes Grey and some Raw Umber to make a shadow tone, and some with White to make a highlight tone. Using a 15mm (⁵⁄₈in) flat brush, block in the window surround using the mid-tone. Depending on your light source (in this case, above left), paint the angled face of the arch and blocks in the highlight tone on one side and in the shadow tone on the other side. Paint the inside return edge of the window lighter on both sides.

9 Mix a range of shades of sky blue using White, Cobalt Blue and Coeruleum Blue. Use a 15mm (⁵⁄₈in) flat brush to cut in around the window, and a 25mm (1in) hog-hair brush to blend the sky blues down from dark to light. You will need two or three coats to achieve a smooth gradation of colour.

10 To some of the mortar colour mixed in step 7, add some more Raw Umber and a little Paynes Grey to make a shadow tone. Use a No. 10 flat brush to add a cast shadow on the mortar, along the bottom and right edge of each block, to give the impression that the stones are standing out from the mortar. Use your finger to smudge the shadows in places.

11 Mix some Raw Umber and a little Paynes Grey with a little water. Using this and the shadow colour mixed in step 10, and Nos. 3 and 5 round pointed brushes, add chips and cracks to the mortar, even painting out some areas, to suggest it has crumbled away. Use your finger to smudge some areas and blend the colours together, so that the lines do not become too defined.

12 Using the shadow colour mixed in step 10 and a No. 3 round pointed brush, paint along the top of the mortar lines in the window surround. Use a straight edge as a guide. Paint the shadow tone to the left of the mortar joint at the top of the arch, as the light source is on the left.

13 Using White and a No. 3 round pointed brush, add sharp highlights to the blocks underneath the joints. Highlight the angled edges to give the corners more definition.

14 Using the dark colour mixed in step 11 and a No. 1 round pointed brush, pick out the fine joints in the surround, again using a straight edge as a guide.

15 Draw the dragon on transfer paper, and transfer the image to the wall. Paint the outlines with Red Oxide and a No. 3 round pointed brush.

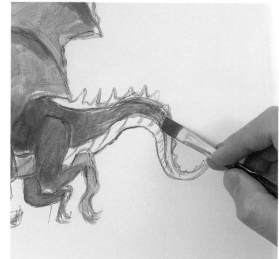

16 Build up layers of colour on the dragon using Red Oxide and Cadmium Orange (adding little or no water) with a No. 10 flat brush.

17 For a bold colour you will need to apply three or more coats, allowing each to dry thoroughly. Mix a little Chromium Oxide Green into the red to make a shadow tone and use this colour with Nos. 1 and 3 round pointed brushes to pick out the finer detailing and shadows, blending the shadow colour into the red. Paint the far wing in the shadow tone to create a feeling of depth. Use Naples Yellow to paint the dragon's belly, and pick out the detailing in Raw Umber with a No. 1 round pointed brush.

18 Block in the objects on the windowsill, using Chromium Oxide Green for the book and mixing White with a little Raw Umber for the pages, Red Oxide and Cadmium Orange for the potion, and the stone colours mixed in step 6 for the pestle and mortar.

19 Mix three or four colours for the dragon's smoke, using White, Flesh Tint and Windsor Violet in varying quantities and adding 1–2 parts water to each colour. Using a 15mm (⅝in) flat brush and the darker colours, stipple a stream of smoke from the dragon's mouth toward the bottom left corner of the window, widening the stream as it goes down. Use a 25mm (1in) hog-hair brush in a circular motion to build up the billows of smoke in the lower part of the window. Alternate between the colours, making the colour deeper at the edge of the window. With the flat brush, cut in around the window edges and the objects and blend into the smoke.

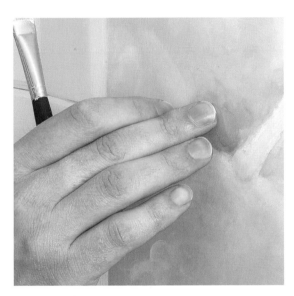

20 Mix White with Cadmium Orange and use Nos. 3 and 5 round pointed brushes to pick out a stream of fire in the centre of the smoke issuing from the dragon's mouth. Deepen the colour of the smoke around the fire to create a bolder contrast. Add some white highlights to the smoke, using the 25mm (1in) hog-hair brush and the same circular motion, and use a No. 5 round pointed brush to pick out the lightest highlights along the top edges of the smoke clouds. Smudge and blend the colours together with your fingers.

21 Add the final details to the book, potion and pestle and mortar. Mix Chromium Oxide Green and Red Oxide to make a shadow tone for the spine of the book. Pick out the gold detailing in Cadmium Yellow using a No. 3 round pointed brush. Use Raw Umber and a little Paynes Grey to define the pages. Use White to pick out the sharp highlights on the potion bottle – the deep smoke colour behind the glass should make them appear quite bold. Build up the pestle and mortar colours so that they are deeper along the bottom and right-hand sides, and inside the bowl. Using some of the stone shadow tone mixed in step 8, paint cast shadows on the windowsill to the bottom and right of the objects.

Carved Toy Chest

THE TOYS FILLING this lovely chest will never clutter up a child's bedroom – at the end of the day they will still be neatly stored away in the box, with all the other playthings of which we can see only tantalizing glimpses.

This is an ideal mural to personalize for a child. You could paint his or her favourite toys peeking out from the top of the box, and instead of the teddy bear relief on the front panel, it could be decorated with the child's own name in carved letters.

The toy chest is painted on the wall, but it is an ideal subject to paint on a panel of medium density fibreboard if you want to be able to change its location. The overall shape of the box can easily be cut out using a jigsaw, and the fixings used to secure it to the wall could be disguised as nails on the hinges.

Carved Toy Chest 107

Palette

Red Oxide

White

Yellow Ochre

Raw Umber

Chromium
Oxide Green

Cadmium Yellow

Cadmium Orange

Cobalt Blue

Paynes Grey

Black

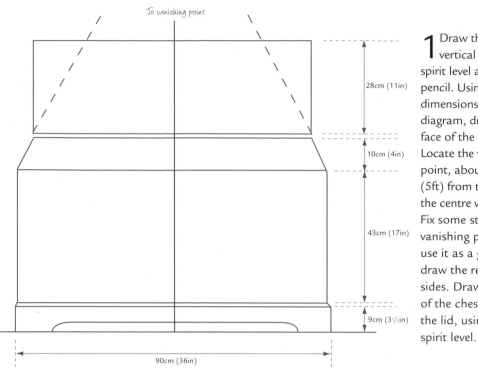

To vanishing point

28cm (11in)

10cm (4in)

43cm (17in)

9cm (3½in)

90cm (36in)

1 Draw the centre vertical using a spirit level and charcoal pencil. Using the dimensions on the diagram, draw the front face of the chest. Locate the vanishing point, about 150cm (5ft) from the floor on the centre vertical. Fix some string at the vanishing point and use it as a guide to draw the receding sides. Draw the back of the chest and the lid, using the spirit level.

2 Build up the detailing, adding the framework to the front, the two metal hinges and the curved base. Divide the lid into three planks. Stand back to check that the chest looks correct to the eye. Once you are satisfied, paint over all the outlines in Red Oxide, using a No. 3 round pointed brush.

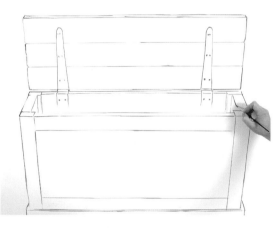

3 Draw one half of the carved teddy on transfer paper, so that the height will fit the front panel of the chest. Transfer the design to the wall, lining it up with the centre vertical, then flip the paper over and trace the other half. Add a few simple star shapes, which can be sketched freehand. Sketch the toys in the chest very loosely on transfer paper, then transfer them to the wall. Try to keep the arrangement balanced – in this case the teddy in the chest is balanced by the boat. Paint over all the outlines in Red Oxide.

4 Mix three colours for the wood. The palest is a mixture of White and Yellow Ochre; add some Raw Umber for the mid-tone, and more Raw Umber for the deepest shade. Mix 2–3 parts water into each, then use a 25mm (1in) hog-hair brush to paint the whole design, alternating between the colours. Use a 15mm (⅝in) flat brush to paint along the edges of the chest.

5 Mix some Raw Umber and Yellow Ochre with about 1 part water. Using a 15mm (⅝in) flat brush, loosely pick out some graining. Add a few knots here and there and then curve the graining around them. Keep the grain running horizontally on the box and lid, but vertically on the sides of the frame. Use the shape of the brush to vary the graining – twisting it slightly to widen or taper the lines. Use some of the colours mixed in step 5 to blend the graining, and do not overdo it – add more later if necessary.

6 Using the graining colour from step 6, pick out the shading and cast shadows – especially on the carved teddy bear and stars. The light source is above left, so the shadows fall to the right and below the relief. Use a No. 10 flat brush for the larger shadows, blending them in slightly using the base wood colours used in step 5. Use a No. 3 round pointed brush to pick out the finer detailing on the teddy's face and paws, and to indicate the stitching. Pick out the shadows cast by the left and top of the frame, and deepen the colour inside the chest around the toys.

7 Block in the toys using a No. 10 and a 15mm (⅝in) flat brush. Mix White, Yellow Ochre and Raw Umber for the teddy and stipple this colour on to suggest a furry texture. Use White for the sail and the teddy colours for the hull of the boat. The ball is painted in stripes of Chromium Oxide Green, Cadmium Orange, Red Oxide and Cobalt Blue – some colours can be used as they are but some will need to be lightened by mixing in some White. Block in the hinges with Paynes Grey and a little White.

8 Mix White with a little Yellow Ochre and Raw Umber, and a little water, to make a highlight tone. Use a No. 10 flat brush to add the highlights to the left side and bottom of the teddy relief and the stars, and a No. 3 round pointed brush to pick out the detailing. Use the same colour to pick out the other highlights on the chest, such as the tops of the planks and the edges of the frame. Mix Raw Umber with a little Paynes Grey and use a No. 3 round pointed brush to pick out the wood joints and a few splits and chips. Build up the colours and forms of the toys, adding cast shadows to the lid. Finally, use blobs of Black to add nail heads to the hinges, and highlight them with White mixed with a little Black, using a No. 3 round pointed brush.

Carved Toy Chest 109

The stonework is made up of uniform blocks. Divide the area into staggered rows of blocks about 43 x 30cm (17 x 12in): it may be easier to work out the arrangement of the stonework first and then fit the window into it.

THIS WINDOW could be used as an alternative design in the Magic Castle Window project. It has a simple arch drawn with one fulcrum, as indicated. The vanishing point, shown in the middle of the window, is used to work out the return angles of all the stonework. Such dramatic stonework would help to create a medieval or Gothic atmosphere in a hallway or dining room.

The stonework is painted in the same colours as the wall in the Magic Castle Window project. Draw the lines lightly with a charcoal pencil, then paint in the mortar and add fine cast shadows depending on the light source — in this case the light comes from the upper right.

If you are carrying the castle theme across a large wall, or even around a whole room, you may want to add some turrets as well as additional windows. To convey the impression that a round turret is protruding from the rest of the wall, curve the lines of blocks upward above eye level and downward below eye level. The further the lines are from the eye level, the more exaggerated the curvature should be. Work out the shape of one side of the top of the turret first. Trace it, and flip it over to trace the other side. Invert the tracing of this curve to draw the foot of the turret.

An simpler option is to paint the turret without blocks, emphasizing the light and shadows to suggest the curvature. Remember to paint a cast shadow on the adjacent stonework.

THIS FAIRYLAND scene is ideal for younger children, as most of the detail and interest is low down at their eye level. The trees form an excellent framing element, with the branches and roots running along the top and bottom of the wall. If you are continuing the scene around more than one wall, the tree trunks can be painted in the corners of the room.

For the tree trunks use a wash mixed from White, Raw Sienna and Raw Umber, deepening the colour toward the edge of the tree to suggest the curvature. Using a No. 3 round pointed brush, pick out the details of the bark, and define the outline, with Raw Umber. You can also blend in a little green in places to bring the tree surface alive.

Paint flowers and toadstools in a very naïve way. You can even paint outlines with a fine round pointed brush to emphasize the individual elements.

The background foliage is stippled on with a 25mm (1in) hog-hair brush, using a light green mixed from White, Chromium Oxide Green and a little Cobalt Blue. Mix in some Leaf Green for the foliage in the middle ground, and more Chromium Oxide Green in the foreground. Deepen the green around the base of the trees and toadstool by adding a little Paynes Grey. For the shoots of grass in the foreground, use a No. 3 round pointed brush with Leaf Green and White, painting short tapering strokes from the bottom up.

Fanciful details like a front door and a window in a tree trunk will help to bring the scene alive, as children imagine who might live inside.

The colours used for the red squirrel are Burnt Sienna, Raw Umber and White.

DRAMATIC DRAPERY creates a theatrical feel for a fantasy landscape. The effect could be carried across a wider wall by adding a few more swags at the top. Such heavy, velvet drapes would also add a passionate touch to a bedroom, or a medieval feel to the window of a dining room.

Sketch one side of the drape first, trace it and flip the tracing to draw the opposite side. Outline the curtains in Red Oxide. Paint a few base coats of Cadmium Red and Red Oxide, or use a red matt emulsion (latex). Mix a little Chromium Oxide Green with the red to paint the shadows in the folds. Mix Cadmium Yellow into the red to pick out the slight highlights on the fabric.

Add the gold fringe using a No. 3 round pointed brush with Naples Yellow. Use short downward strokes, trying to keep them all of a uniform size, and leave some of the deep red showing through the tassels to help define them. Retouch the red later if necessary. You could also add touches of Gold acrylic on top of the Naples Yellow.

If you have an interest in calligraphy or a good handwriting style, you can use it as part of a mural scene. The elements in this scene frame an unrolled scroll, on which you could inscribe a nursery rhyme, lines from a fairytale or a suitable quotation.

Use various mixes of White, Yellow Ochre, Raw Sienna and Raw Umber for the scroll. Water the colours down and build up layers of washes to give the look of old parchment.

Add highlights using lighter colours and White — the highlights on the book spines can be painted using a small flat brush and stippling horizontally down the side of each spine.

Both shelves, and the books on the upper shelf, have the same vanishing point. Plan these first, before adding the toy images. Outline the whole design in Red Oxide using a No. 3 round pointed brush.

A TROMPE l'oeil shelf is an ideal solution if the available wall space is limited and the wall is painted in a plain colour. You may wish to give the wall a fresh coat of paint before you start. The toys shown here are ideal for a child, but the shelf could be painted in any room of the house, and hold books (see left), flowers (page 46), a collection of sea shells (page 90) and any number of trompe l'oeil items. Flick through the design libraries for more inspiration.

To begin, block in the main areas of colour, watering down the paint only slightly, and using suitable bright colours. Paint all the areas of the same colour simultaneously (such as the red on the soldier and the wooden train) to help knit the painting together. As you build up the colours, begin to differentiate between the light and shadowed sides of each toy to bring out their forms. Deepen the shadows where the toys sit on the shelf.

You will need to include cast shadows behind a trompe l'oeil shelf, so you will need some of the colour used to paint the wall to mix the shadow colours: you may wish to give the wall a fresh coat of paint before you start. For this light yellow wall, the shadow tone is made by adding very small amounts of Windsor Violet and Paynes Grey. Use some of the original wall colour to diffuse the edges of the shadows so they do not become too harsh. Mix some white with the original wall colour and blend in a little of this up to the shadows to emphasize them.

You can trace the toys on these two pages, or sketch real toys belonging to the child for whom you are painting the mural.

THIS STYLIZED space scene is inspired by 1950s science fiction, and is perfect for budding young astonauts. The starry sky would also be fitting for a bedroom ceiling.

Sketch the large planet using a pencil tied to a piece of string taped low on the wall. Mix three colours for the sky: Black and Windsor Violet, Black and Cobalt Blue, and plain Black. Alternate between the colours and blend them into each other on the wall. You will need at least two coats to achieve the dark, rich colour of the sky. To create the hazy nebulae, mix Cobalt Blue with a little White, and Windsor Violet with a little White; thin with 2—3 parts water. Use a large decorator's brush to stipple some faint cloudy shapes, fizzling them out towards the edges. Keep stippling to soften the colour and remove any obvious brush marks.

To create the eclipse, a rare phenomenon that appeals
to astromomers young and old, draw round a circular object
(a plate is ideal) and paint in the white crescent with a No. 5 round
pointed brush, blending it out into the dark sky and stippling in more of the cloudy
effects. Redraw the circle and paint it in pure Black, using a 15mm (⅝in) flat brush.
The stars are blobs of White, very slightly watered down and applied with Nos. 1 and 3 round
pointed brushes. Keep the spacing random and try to cluster stars in places, especially inside the nebulae.
Paint the planet in the foreground using mixtures of Chromium Oxide Green, Burnt Sienna and White.

Suppliers

UK

Craig and Rose plc
Halbeath Industrial Estate
Crossgates Road
Dunfermline
Fife KY11 7EG
tel: 01383 740 000
fax: 01383 740 010
email: enquiries@craigandrose.com
dead flat varnish and other specialist paints and brushes

Daler-Rowney Ltd
Bracknell
Berkshire RG12 8ST
tel: 01344 424621
fax: 01344 485511
www.daler-rowney.com
artists' materials including acrylics, oils, gouache and brushes

Polyvine Limited
Marybrook Street
Berkeley
Gloucestershire GL13 9AA
tel: 0870 787 3710
fax: 0870 787 3709
email: info@polyvine.co.uk
flat and satin varnish and other clear coats, decorative paints, woodcare products and industrial coatings

Royal Brush Manufacturing (UK) Ltd
Block 3 Unit 3
Wednesbury Trading Estate
Bilston Rd
Wednesbury
West Midlands WS10 7JN
tel: 0121 556 8422
fax: 0121 556 9988
email: uk@royalbrush.com
artists' brushes and paints

Winsor & Newton
Whitefriars Avenue
Harrow
Middlesex HA3 5RH
England
tel: 0208 427 4343
fax: 0208 863 7177
www.winsornewton.com
artists' materials including acrylics, oils, gouache and brushes

US

Daler-Rowney
2 Corporate Drive
Cranbury
New Jersey 08512
tel: 609 655 5252
fax: 609 655 5825
www.daler-rowney.com/usa
artists' materials including acrylics, oils, gouache and brushes

Polyvine Inc
500 Palm Street #22
West Palm Beach
Florida 33401
tel: 561 820 1500
fax: 561 820 1575
email: polyvine@earthlink.net
flat and satin varnish and other clear coats, decorative paints, woodcare products and industrial coatings

Royal & Langnickel Brush Mfg Inc
6707 Broadway
Merrillville
Indiana 46410
tel: 800 247 2211/219 660 4170
fax: 219 660 4181
email: customerservice@royalbrush.com
artists' brushes and paints

Winsor & Newton
PO Box 1396
Piscataway,
New Jersey 08855
tel: 800 445 4278
fax: 732 562 0941
www.winsornewton.com
artists' materials including acrylics, oils, gouache and brushes

Online

Muralsplus, developed by Martin Alan Hirsch, is an online resource for faux painting enthusiasts, muralists, and decorative painters looking for ideas or wanting to increase their level of expertise.
www.muralsplus.com

ABOUT THE AUTHOR

Christopher Westall is an established decorative artist with over fifteen years' experience painting trompe l'oeil scenes and murals. He currently works on murals and trompe l'oeils for a range of private clients and business premises. This is his second book for David & Charles, the first being *Trompe l'Oeil Interiors*. Christopher lives in Essex, England, with his wife Jayne and their two children, Adam and Hannah. Further examples of his work can be seen at www.mural-design.com

ACKNOWLEDGMENTS

I would like to thank everybody who has helped in putting this book together – especially Fiona Eaton, Ali Myer and Jennifer Proverbs.

Special thanks to Karl Adamson for the photography and the long days shooting (especially the final day), and also to my patrons, for allowing us to photograph their commissions, and for letting me loose on their walls in the first place.

Index